WAR DEPARTMENT BASIC FIELD MANUAL
FM 70-15

This manual supersedes FM 31-15, 18 September 1941, including C 1, 16 April 1942, and C2, 29 September, 1942.

OPERATIONS IN SNOW AND EXTREME COLD

WAR DEPARTMENT • NOVEMBER 1944

WILDSIDE PRESS

WAR DEPARTMENT
WASHINGTON 25, D.C., 4 NOVEMBER 1944.

FM 70–15, Operations in Snow and Extreme Cold, is published for the information and guidance of all concerned.

[A. G. 300.7 (21 Sep 44).]

BY ORDER OF THE SECRETARY OF WAR:

G. C. MARSHALL
Chief of Staff.

OFFICIAL:

J. A. ULIO,
Major General,
The Adjutant General.

DISTRIBUTION:

Continental: As prescribed in paragraph 9a, FM 21–6; Oversea: T of Opns (2) ; Base C (2) ; Island C (2) ; Def C (2) ; Base Sectors (2) ; Depts (2) ; SvC (2) ; in addition to the foregoing oversea distribution, troops located in Alaskan Dept and NW SvC will be distributed to on the following basis: Armies (5) ; Corps (5) ; D (5) ; B (5) ; R (5) ; Bn (5) ; C (5) .

For explanation of symbols, see FM 21–6.

CONTENTS

This manual supersedes FM 31–15, 18 September 1941, including C 1, 16 April 1942; and C 2, 29 September 1942.

Chapter 1

GENERAL

1. Basic Principles.

a. Military operations conducted under conditions of snow and extreme cold follow the same basic principles as do operations under other conditions. The differences lie in the tactical and logistical limitations imposed by the adverse climatic conditions and in the special equipment, training, and procedures necessary to overcome these limitations. Failure to equip and train troops properly for operations in extreme cold before beginning operations leads directly to failure of the operations themselves.

b. The principles and doctrine described in this manual are applicable to operations conducted under conditions of snow and extreme cold in any type of terrain. They are not limited to operations in those portions of the world which are usually designated as "Alpine" or "Arctic."

c. Additional information on operations in extreme cold is contained in TM 1–240.

d. All temperatures cited in this manual are expressed in degrees Fahrenheit.

2. Major Problems.

Four major problems present themselves for solution in operations in snow and extreme cold: keeping men and animals warm; moving troops across snow and ice; transporting and preserving supplies

For military terms not defined in this manual, see TM 20–205.

and equipment; and preventing the malfunctioning of weapons and equipment.

a. KEEPING MEN AND ANIMALS WARM. (1) Men are subject to chilling, frostbite, freezing, and snow blindness. When cold, they are less alert. Without proper shelter and covering they lose sleep and weaken. Their fingers may become numb from cold, resulting in poor handling of their weapons. They seek sheltered locations and huddle together for warmth. There are occasions requiring violent exertion which result in their becoming overheated, followed by periods of inactivity during which they may freeze. They lose articles of equipment in deep snow. When the air is still and dry, they are likely to consider the temperature higher than it actually is and become careless in their precautions against frostbite.

(2) Animals suffer from cold and frosted lungs. They may require hot food, warmed water, prepared beds and shelter, although sled dogs survive without these items. Animal food consumption rises. Horses need nose shields and frequent rubdowns.

b. MOVING TROOPS ACROSS SNOW AND ICE. Deep snow and drifts impede progress both on and off roads. Movement of even a few feet from cleared areas becomes impossible without the use of snow-crossing equipment. Ordinary wheeled vehicles are useless, and armored track-laying vehicles experience difficulty, in operating in snow over 18 inches deep. Troops unable to cross snow and ice are caught in a continuous defile on cleared roads or trails. Snowshoes, skis, crampons or ice creepers, and oversnow vehicles—snow tractors and motorized toboggans—are essential if personnel are to be employed advantageously in executing tactical decisions.

c. TRANSPORTING AND PRESERVING SUPPLIES AND EQUIPMENT. (1) Supplies and equipment assume a relatively greater importance in cold than they normally do, as life is more immediately dependent upon their adequacy and uninterrupted delivery. The bulk of supplies, particularly fuel, rations and forage, becomes greater in cold weather, while at the same time the means for handling this bulk are more narrowly limited.

(2) The same restrictions which deep snow places on the movement of troops are equally applicable to the movement of supplies and equipment. Rear area roads and railroads must be maintained and cleared. Roads in forward areas, if they exist, form dangerous defiles. Carrying parties and man-drawn sleds exhaust man power and are inefficient.

(3) Certain items of supply freeze in extreme cold. Means of prevention must be devised.

d. MALFUNCTIONING OF WEAPONS AND EQUIPMENT. Motors require special starting and maintenance techniques; lubricants stiffen; gasoline and chemicals vaporize less readily; condensation of water in fuel tanks and carburetors occurs; oil and fuel fail to flow through pipes; water jackets freeze; springs become brittle and difficult to compress; steel breaks more easily; frost fogs windshields and the lenses of optical instruments; rubber sometimes cracks; batteries fail; ice collects in bores of weapons; mechanisms improperly lubricated do not function properly; the ballistics of weapons are modified; explosives become unstable; frost and ice form on aircraft wings; gears and unions of dissimilar metals bind.

e. SOLUTION OF PROBLEMS. For a solution of the above problems, upon which the success of operations in snow and extreme cold depends, the following conditions must obtain: First, there must be available an adequate quantity of clothing, equipment, and supplies suitable for use under such conditions; second, officers and men must be thoroughly trained in taking care of themselves and their supplies and equipment, keeping themselves and their transportation mobile, and keeping their weapons functioning. Training should be conducted under field conditions similar to those to be encountered in later tactical and logistical operations.

Chapter 2

RATIONS AND THEIR PREPARATION

Section I. GENERAL

3. Importance of Food.

Troops lose military efficiency when they are uncomfortably cold. Regular sustaining hot food and drink are prime factors in maintaining body warmth. Food supplies both heat and energy. More food is required by the body in extreme cold weather than in a temperate climate for the following reasons:

a. More energy must be expended to maintain normal body warmth.

b. More energy is used as the result of increased activity.

c. More energy is needed because of the additional weight of arctic clothing and equipment.

d. More energy is required to overcome the increased obstacles caused by snow and ice.

4. Heat Generating Foods.

From a fuel or energy standpoint there are three principal nutrients: protein, carbohydrate, and fat.

a. PROTEIN. Protein is present chiefly in meats, fish, eggs, and milk. It supplies heat and energy in about the same amount as carbohydrate, but it is used primarily as a builder and repairer of muscle tissue. It is needed by the body in about the same amount in frigid as in temperate climates.

b. CARBOHYDRATE. Carbohydrate is found in such foods as sugars, cereals, fruits, and vegetables. The energy supplied by carbohydrate is produced speedily because of the readiness with which the body consumes sugars and starches. In extremely cold weather, the body requires increased quantities of carbohydrates.

c. FAT. Fat is supplied by animal foods such as meat, milk, butter, and lard, and by vegetable foods such as cottonseed, corn, and olive oils. Fat requires a longer time to digest than carbohydrate or protein, but gives off about twice as much heat. Fat is extremely important in the arctic diet because when stored in the body it can be used as a source of future heat and energy. It has good heat insulating qualities, and it tends to delay the sensations of hunger.

5. Food Deficiency Diseases.

Scurvy and beriberi are two diseases caused by deficiency of necessary nutrients and may develop after a number of months, if they are not guarded against. Vitamin C (ascorbic acid) is considered a specific for the prevention and cure of scurvy, as is Vitamin B1 (thiamin) for beriberi. When these vitamins are lacking from the diet, the synthetic substitutes should be provided.

6. Water.

Obtaining sufficient water for cooking and drinking purposes is an important consideration in cold regions. Running water is used whenever available. Glacier water is usually clean enough if the sediment is given a little time to settle. Frequently, however, snow or ice will have to be melted to obtain water. Ice is preferred because it is denser than snow and hence yields more water for a given volume. When snow must be used, wet or frozen snow is better than powder snow. Unless snow is melted properly the bottom of the container may be burned. Pack about $\frac{1}{2}$-inch of snow in the bottom of the cooking vessel and melt it completely. Then add additional snow from time to time in amounts small enough so that the contents are always slush.

a. DRINKING WATER. Water obtained from running streams, lakes, and ponds may ordinarily be considered safe for drinking and cooking. However, if any doubt exists as to the purity of the source, or if river water is used, the water must be made safe for use by boiling, or by treating it with halazone or iodine.

b. FILLING THE CANTEEN. Water is rarely carried in the canteen at temperature much below freezing. When water is carried, the canteen should be filled only three-fourths full, leaving enough space for the water to expand without breaking the canteen in the event the water should freeze solid. The canteen may be wrapped in the sleeping bag or a garment for insulation.

c. EATING SNOW. In the absence of drinking water small quantities of snow may be eaten while troops are warm or on the move. It is better to place a small piece of ice or compressed snow in the mouth than to suck it, otherwise the lips may become chapped. If the soldier is cold, or hot and tired, he should not eat snow. Snow should never be swallowed in lumps as this may chill the stomach. It should never be eaten in large quantities as it will materially reduce body temperature, and may cause severe chafing of the lips. It is generally better to eat a little snow often, than to wait until one is thirsty and eat too much.

7. Other Liquids.

a. HOT DRINKS. Hot drinks, such as tea, coffee, or cocoa should be served with meals, in addition to hot soups. On marches it is often desirable to take less frequent but longer rests than the usual 10 minutes per hour. In this way men can prepare a hot drink of tea, coffee, or even soup while they are resting. A 5- or 10-minute break which does not allow time for the preparation of hot drinks may, during very cold weather, do more harm than good.

b. ALCOHOLIC DRINKS. It is dangerous to take alcohol in any form during exposure to extreme cold. Alcohol causes the blood vessels of the skin to become dilated. Much blood flows close to the surface of the body and a rapid heat loss results. In this way a man can get a false sensation of warmth, while actually he may be lowering his body temperature to a dangerous degree. In an emergency, however, as when a man is saved from starvation or rescued from exposure, an alcoholic drink may start him on the road to recovery. Such cases should be fed only with liquids, administered frequently in small quantities. When strength begins to return, solid food may be allowed in moderation.

8. Heated Foods.

Whenever possible, food should be served hot. Since cold mess equipment soon chills food it is desirable to have mess gear made of some material which is a poor heat conductor. However, if such equipment is not available, the food can be eaten at once from the container in which it was cooked. If feasible, meals should be served in heated tents or shelters, and arrangements made so that men will not have to sit on the snow. If tents are used it is desirable that a separate tent for cooking be provided; if the men cook in the tents in which they sleep there will be a large accumulation of frost on clothing and equipment, with resulting discomfort and possible danger. If tents are not available, meals should be eaten in sheltered woods or behind ice or snow windbreaks. Preparation of meals must always be carried out efficiently and . rapidly, or the men are likely to become chilled while waiting.

9. Preservation of Foods.

a. The use of perishable foods under cold weather conditions will normally be small even in stabilized situations. When fresh foods can be obtained, however, and are to be used immediately, they should not be frozen. Freezing and thawing sometimes results in giving the food an undesirable appearance. Vegetables which are eaten without cooking, such as tomatoes, cucumbers, celery, radishes, and lettuce should never be allowed to freeze because freezing wilts them and makes them flabby instead of crisp. Other perishables, such as fresh meat, eggs, raw potatoes, and vegetables which require cooking may be allowed to freeze without injury and may be stored indefinitely if kept frozen hard. Once thawed, however, they spoil quickly, and subsequent freezing does not restore them. Accordingly they should be kept frozen until they are to be used, and, when thawed, should be eaten immediately.

b. Canned Foods. Canned foods may be allowed to freeze without injury to the contents, but should not be subjected to repeated freezing and thawing because this may impair the quality of the food. If possible, canned fruits and vegetables which have been frozen should be thawed gradually in a warm room 75° to 85° F. Generally, freezing of the contents of a can will not cause straining of can seams since the increase in bulk is somewhat compensated for by the head space in the can. While the bursting of cans from freezing is unlikely, most canned items will bulge at the ends when frozen. This does not necessarily mean that the contents are spoiled by fermentation and decomposition. The way to tell whether the can is spoiled is to allow the contents to thaw in the unopened can. If the contents are good, the can will return to its normal shape.

Section II. RATIONS

10. Standard Rations.

Troops will normally be supplied with field ration A or B while in garrison or under stabilized battle conditions in rear areas, and with one of the packaged rations while in combat. There is no standard ration which is designed exclusively for operations in snow and extreme cold.

a. FIELD RATIONS A AND B. Field rations A and B are almost identical except that non-perishable foods are provided in B to replace similar perishable items in A. Menus are adapted from a master menu supplied by the appropriate department or theater quartermaster. These menus take into consideration the extra fuel required by men operating in cold weather.

b. PACKAGED RATIONS. Where field ration A or B cannot be provided in rear areas, and where individual combat rations are needed, the most appropriate of the packaged rations will be provided.

(1) *10-in-1 ration.* The 10-in-1 ration is designed for feeding small groups. It is intended that the meals be heated, but in an emergency they can be eaten cold.

(2) *C ration.* The C ration consists of food packed in hermetically sealed cans, containing meat products, biscuits, confections, and a beverage. Each ration also has an additional packet con-

taining cigarettes, matches, chewing gum, halazone tablets, and toilet tissue. The ration was designed to provide a man with one meat and one biscuit unit per meal. The ration will supply him with 3,150 calories (heat units).

(3) *K ration.* The K ration consists of 3 one-meal packages designed as breakfast, dinner, and supper for one man. Each of the 3 units contains a can of meat, meat and egg product, or cheese. In addition, each unit contains biscuits, a confection, a beverage, chewing gum, and cigarettes.

(4) *D ration.* The D ration is a concentrated emergency ration consisting of three 4-ounce chocolate bars. It is intended to be used when no other ration is available. It can also be issued as a supplement to other packaged rations, to be eaten as an added confection or as a hot chocolate drink.

11. Ration Increases.

The definition of a ration as food for one man for one day should not be misconstrued to mean that if a man requires more food than that provided by one ration, it cannot be made available to him. *The fundamental consideration of providing for troops is that they be adequately fed at all times.* Under conditions of extremely cold weather or hard work, when the body requires larger quantities of heat and energy-producing foods, it may be necessary to supply the individual soldier with food in greater amounts than those fixed upon as the normal requirement. For example, it may be necessary to provide a man with 4 or 5 meal units of the K ration instead of with 3, or with 8 or 10 instead of the usual 6 cans of C ration per day. Similarly, it may be necessary to provide a group of only 6 or 8 men with a complete 10–in–1 ration during operations in snow and extreme cold. Appropriate commanders are permitted to authorize increased issues where the necessity for them exists.

Section III. PREPARATION OF RATIONS

12. Cooking in Garrison.

Cooking in garrison and in rear areas under cold weather conditions will normally be similar to cooking under any other climatic conditions. As troops move forward toward the active battle front, soldiers usually will be required to cook and eat in smaller groups. Individual cooking equipment will then be brought into use, and small group messing technique will be employed.

13. Individual Cooking Equipment.

One-burner gasoline cooking stoves are issued for the use of mobile troops who prepare and cook their own food. These stoves are easy to manage, burn little fuel, and are light to carry. Operating instructions for these stoves, and complete information on all individual cooking equipment, will be found in TM 10–275 and 10–400. If extremely low temperatures are anticipated it is desirable to employ some solid fuel, or a primer type of gasoline stove. At outposts where fires are not permissible, thermos containers are advantageous.

14. Small Group Cooking.

a. SIZE OF GROUPS. Cooking should always be done in as large a group as the situation permits, for convenience in preparation of the meal and for conservation of fuel. Even if there is plenty of fuel, the pooling of a number of stoves is advantageous. At the beginning, all of the stoves will be needed to melt snow quickly, after which each stove can be used to prepare a particular part of the meal, or held in readiness for use as a substitute for any stove which may fail during the preparation of the meal. This last is especially important because the fuel capacity of the stoves is limited.

b. Cooking Hints. The following suggestions will be helpful:

(1) Thaw out frozen meat before cooking. Partly frozen meat may cook on the outside while the center remains raw.

(2) Cook vegetables only until they are tender. Overcooking reduces their vitamin content and wastes fuel. Use only a small amount of water to get the best flavor from vegetables and to prevent extensive loss of vitamins. Drink the water used for cooking vegetables, or use it in soup. It is unnecessary to thaw out frozen vegetables completely; simply drop the small frozen pieces into boiling water.

.(3) Heat canned foods only enough to warm them. Cooking canned foods is unnecessary and wastes fuel.

(4) Dip frozen potatoes in hot water and then scrape off the skins for easier peeling. Before they have thawed drop them in boiling water one by one so the water keeps boiling. Cut them up to shorten cooking time.

c. Mess Gear. When the meal is finished, mess gear must be cleaned thoroughly in boiling water in order to remove all grease and other material which tends to cling to the kit. Mess gear which is not thoroughly clean may cause diarrhea.

Chapter 3
CLOTHING

15. References.
Complete information of the use, care and maintenance of cold weather clothing is found in TM 10–275.

16. Principles of Insulation.
Substances which offer little resistance to the transference of heat are known as good *conductors;* those which resist it are said to be good *insulators.* Suitable cold weather clothing is not warm in itself; it is merely a good insulator and a poor conductor of heat. The heat of the body is held in by the clothing, and prevented from escaping into the atmosphere. Since still air is an excellent insulator, the best cold weather clothes are those which entrap a considerable amount of air. The warmth of a woolen sweater lies mainly in the thousands of tiny air cells between the woolen fibers; fur is warm because of the air trapped among the hairs. Several thin layers of cloth are better than one thick, heavy, matted piece of material, for air pockets can form between the layers.

17. Prevention of Perspiration.
Clothing which has become damp is a poor insulating agent. Perspiration is a common source of moisture in clothing. Physical exercise will cause perspiration even in coldest weather. To prevent excessive perspiration, which results in damp clothing and a consequent chilling and frostbite of specific areas, precautions must be taken to insure that troops remove or loosen outer garments at the start

of exercise. These garments should be kept dry in the packs, and located so that they may be worn during breaks and at the end of the exercise.

18. Essential Characteristics of Cold Weather Clothing.

a. All cold weather clothing, both outer and inner, should be—

(1) Loose-fitting.

(2) Clean.

(3) Dry.

b. Outer clothing should be—

(1) *Windproof,* to prevent displacement of the insulating air held in air-pockets in the clothing.

(2) *Water-repellent,* to keep light rain and snow from penetrating to the inner clothing. *Waterproof* clothing should not be worn in freezing weather, since the moisture from the body will collect on the inside and turn to frost.

c. Inner clothing should consist of several layers of some good spongy insulating material, such as wool or pile.

19. Responsibility for Wear of Proper Clothing.

The types of clothing made available for wear in cold weather in any particular area are determined by higher headquarters as a result of previous planning. In the interests of uniformity the outer garments to be worn should be prescribed by the unit commander. However, individuals vary as to the amount of clothing needed for adequate warmth. Each man should be aware of his individual needs and govern his wearing of undergarments so as to prevent both overheating and chilling. Unit leaders should be aware of the danger of requiring uniformity of undergarments as this will cause overheating or chilling of certain personnel and will

15

result in ineffectives. All commanders must be alert to the needs of the situation, and should take the necessary steps to insure that the proper amount of clothing is worn and is modified to avoid perspiration while working, or chilling after work ceases.

Chapter 4

SHELTER AND HEAT

Section I. SHELTER

20. General.

The need for shelter is particularly acute in extreme cold and is instinctively sought by men and animals.

  a. Cold-weather shelter should provide an adequate windbreak, insulation against loss of heat from the interior of the shelter, a source of heat where posssible, and drying racks for clothing and equipment.

  b. Shelters should be sited to protect personnel and equipment from drifting snow and prevailing winds.

  c. Shelters may be improvised from materials at hand or transported. Improvised cold weather shelters may be constructed from snow, logs, boughs, sod, or any other material at hand in sufficient quantity. Transported shelters are usually tents, but may be prefabricated houses or huts. They should be light, compact, durable, and easily erected and disassembled by unskilled workers.

21. Buildings.

Where buildings are available, they should be used to the greatest extent possible. Isolated buildings capable of being heated can be used to good advantage for drying wet or sweaty clothing and footgear.

22. Tentage.

Medium-sized tents are better than small ones, since the body heat of a number of men together raises the inside temperature. A six-man tent may be improvised from double-ended shelter-halves. Such a tent provides space near the peak where clothing can be hung to dry. Floor cloths should be provided to keep bedding off the ground. The two-man mountain tent, which has a fixed floor cloth, is a very satisfactory tent, and is quickly and easily erected. The pyramidal tent of the type normally issued is not entirely satisfactory for operations in cold weather because of its weight.

23. Prefabricated Shelters.

Prefabricated shelters are made in sections and are readily erected. They are made of composition board, plywood or galvanized steel. They usually accommodate six to eight men, and may be heated by wood, coal, or oil stoves.

Section II. SHELTER IN TIMBER

24. General.

a. The location of a bivouac area in timber gives protective concealment unless the timber area stands by itself so obviously as to indicate to the enemy that it is the probable location of the bivouac. Timber containing a high percentage of evergreen trees is the most desirable type, as the trees themselves provide the maximum amount of shelter, as well as the best source of building materials, fuel, and bedding.

b. For small or widely dispersed units, it is usually practicable to cut sufficient boughs for bedding without materially reducing the overhead cover provided by the timber. Wherever possible, lower branches only should be removed. Small branches may be stripped from boughs too large for bedding. When sufficient boughs cannot be safely

removed, straw, hay, newspapers, pasteboard from
ration and ammunition containers, or similar material, can be used to good advantage.

25. Types of Shelter.

a. Snow Shelter Trench (fig. 1). (1) This
form of shelter is easy to make and to conceal, and
is fairly comfortable. A snow trench larger than the
sleeping bag is excavated below the surface of the
snow, but not to the ground. Boughs are cut in
sufficient quantity to provide a layer several inches
thick after compression by the sleeper's weight. The
bough bed should be thick enough to prevent the
sleeping bag or any other equipment from touching
the snow at any point. The boughs are covered by
a shelter half, any extra clothing is placed evenly
on top of the shelter half, and the sleeping bag is
placed upon the layer of clothing. An access pit
will prevent loose snow from being knocked into
the sleeping bag upon entering or leaving.

(2) The snow shelter trench may be made more
elaborate by the addition of a roof of boughs, or an

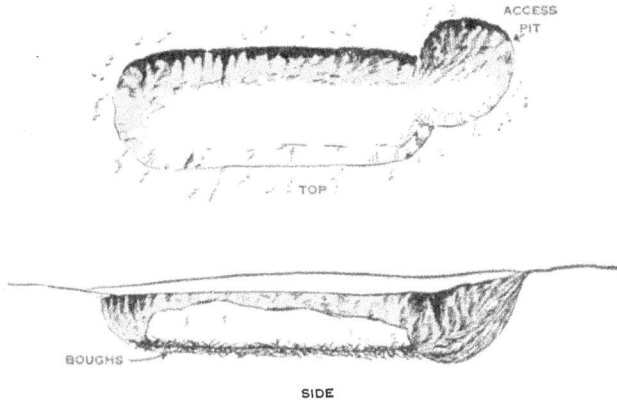

ACCESS
PIT

TOP

BOUGHS

SIDE

Figure 1. Snow shelter trench.

19

improvised stove placed at one end of the trench.

b. LEAN-TO (fig. 2). (1) The lean-to is the standard timber shelter. It is of considerable value when the tactical situation permits the use of open fires. It may be constructed in various sizes to house two or more men and their equipment. The small lean-to permits the use of a small fire and it is warmer than a large one. Snow is first tramped down or cleared from the selected site. Two large uprights (AA) are erected or selected in place, and one large transverse piece (C') laid in their forks or lashed to them. Back pieces (B) are placed at intervals along the transverse member (C') with their ends resting on the snow or ground. These pieces should have several inches of their branches left on them to support the cross members (C). Boughs are then placed on the cross members by hooking their branches to the cross members, and the roof thatched. Side members (D) may be leaned against the roof and the sides thatched.

(2) The shelter can be improved by the use of a fire (and fire base, if in deep snow) and a reflector (fig. 3). The fire base should be formed of two layers of green logs larger than the fire itself. These will keep the fire from sinking into the snow. The

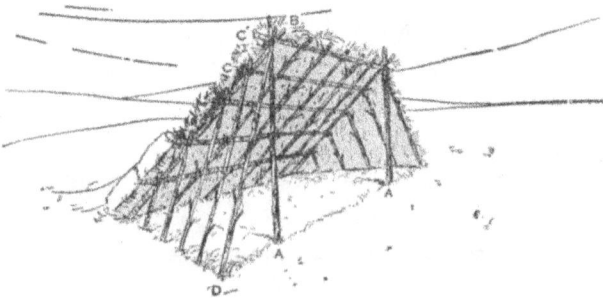

Figure 2. Single lean-to.

reflector should also be built of green logs and placed on the opposite side of the fire from the opening of the lean-to. It will reflect heat into the lean-to as shown in figure 3.

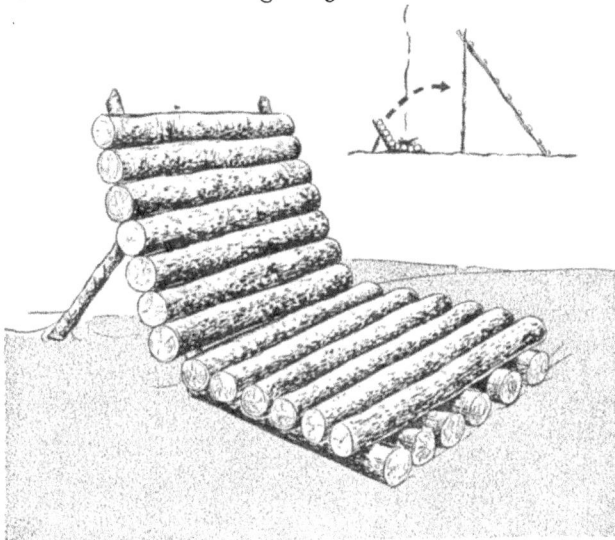

Figure 3. Fire base and reflector.

(3) Two lean-tos may be built facing one another or at right angles to one another with a fire between; or with two facing each other and two others facing each other across the open ends of the space between the first two.

c. FALLEN TREE SHELTER (fig. 4). A tree purposely cut, or a fallen dead tree, may be thatched to make a low tent-like shelter. Using a newly cut evergreen, the branches on the under side should be trimmed off and an excavation made in the snow to provide necessary space. The trimmed branches may be used to prepare a thick bough lining. Branches and boughs from the upper side can

21

be used to thatch the sides. Fallen dead trees of hard consistency, and not rotted, can be made into a shelter by wattling and thatching the sides. *Wattling* is the making of a framework by interweaving twigs.

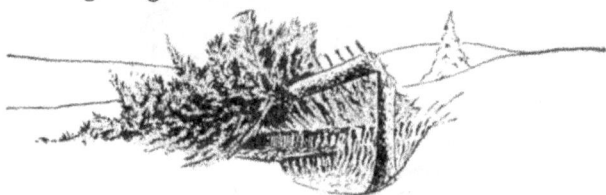

Figure 4. Fallen tree shelter.

d. STANDING-TREE SHELTER (fig. 5). Standing evergreen trees may be used for shelter by wattling and thatching the sides. Snow may be cleared and the interior lined with boughs. In deep snow this type of shelter provides exceptionally good concealment.

Figure 5. Standing tree shelter.

22

e. OTHER TYPES. Other types of shelter, or modifications of those already described, such as double lean-tos, hillside huts, wigwams, and tree tents, may also be constructed, according to the ingenuity of the builder and the materials available.

Section III. SHELTER WITHOUT TIMBER

26. General.

a. On treeless terrain or on terrain in which trees and woods must be avoided for tactical reasons, shelters must be constructed without timber. In such cases, shelters may be provided by the use of snow, sod, earth, rocks, vehicles, canvas and other equipment, and excavation.

b. Snow is a very good insulator and when available should be used as a means of keeping shelters warm. It is, however, a poor ventilating agent. All snow or snow-covered shelters should have some provision for ventilation. This is particularly necessary if a light or fire is to be used in the shelter.

c. In many areas of North America and Asia extreme cold without snow or with very scanty snow is found. This condition obtains in the arid and semiarid deserts, steppes, and plains where vegetation is scant. Winds are apt to be very strong, and vehicles and equipment must be used as components of shelters and as windbreaks whenever possible.

27. Types of Shelter.

a. TENTAGE. Tents should be dug into the snow when pitched in open country. Tents without floors must be banked to prevent entry of wind under them thus causing their collapse by ballooning. When the mountain tent is used the door should remain open, in order to avoid condensation of moisture inside of the tent. Tents should be pitched so that the entrance is at right angles to the direction of the wind in order to keep the doorways free from drifts. All available appropriate material should be used to build insulating sleeping pads inside the tent.

b. SNOW CAVES (fig. 6). Snow caves can be made easily where the snow blanket is deep and has lain in place long enough to become compact. Caves are frequently made in the sides of roads or trails; when entered from a flat surface, they are provided with access pits. If a source of heat is placed in a snow cave, the latter is likely to become damp and the roof may fall in. A vent in the roof at its highest point provides ventilation and retards melting. In order to maintain a higher inside temperature, all caves should have sleeping benches above the level of the entry. When possible, the entrance should slope upward to help keep in the heat. This is most easily done when the cave is dug into a hillside.

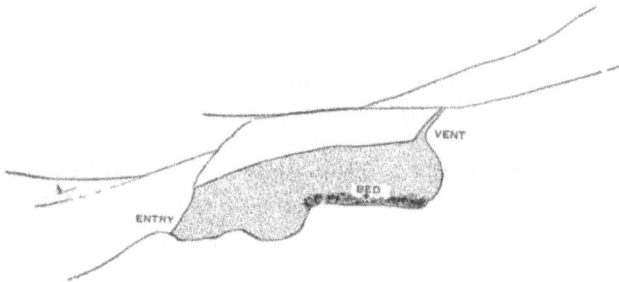

Figure 6. Snow cave.

c. SNOW HOUSES. For a description of snow houses (igloos), see section III, appendix I.

d. WINDBREAKS. (1) *Snow walls* (fig. 7). Blocks cut from compact snow can be made into a windbreak. Such windbreaks are practical only when the snow is very hard; otherwise bad drifts will pile up. Sleeping bags will wet through if the sleeper is in the open. Tents are likely to collapse from the weight of the snow.

Figure 7. Snow wall.

(2) *Vehicles and sleds* (fig. 8). When camp is made, motor vehicles and sleds can be parked to form windbreaks. The open spaces under a motor vehicle may be filled with snow blocks, and tarpaulins erected, using the vehicle as the support for one side. Sleds turned on edge and covered by tarpaulins make excellent shelters from the wind. If vehicles and tarpaulins are used as shown, individual tentage may be used for a sleeping pad.

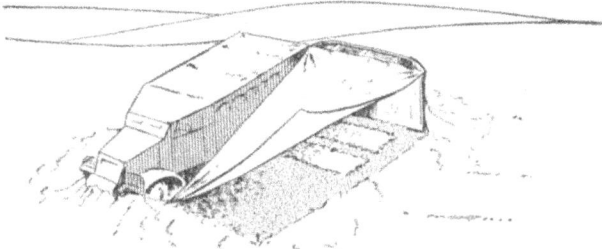

Figure 8. Motor vehicles and sleds as shelter.

e. SOD HOUSES. In stabilized situations, construction of sod houses may be desirable. One type of construction is shown in figure 9.

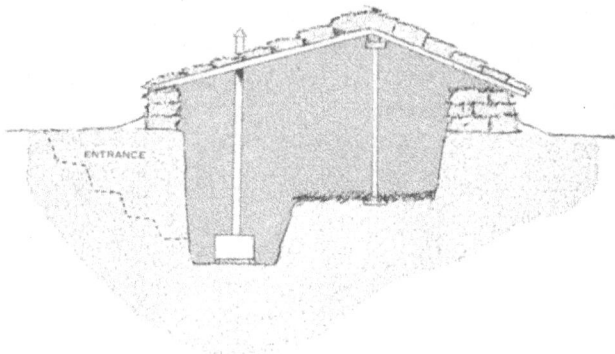

Figure 9. Sod house: cut and cover type.

f. SNOW HOLE. The snow hole is an individual burrow in snow with loose snow plugging the entrance. It may be used by soldiers halted by enemy fire in severe weather or by units advancing by night over open country which is under enemy observation by day. Unless troops using the snow-hole method have good water-repellent clothing, use of the hole will be dangerous.

g. SNOW-SHELTER TRENCH (fig. 10). The most quickly built and most easily concealed individual shelter is the snow shelter trench. The method of construction is in general the same as in timber. The difference lies in the absence of boughs for insulating the sleeping bag. In lieu of boughs, the packboard or rucksack should be placed where it supports the hips and torso. Snow shoes or skis, placed upside down with air space between them and the snow, will insulate the legs. Folded packs, waterproof bags, etc., are placed under the shoulders. The tentage and insulating pad, if carried, are placed over these and the sleeping bag placed on top.

26

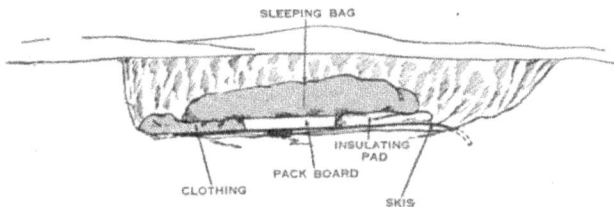

Figure 10. Snow shelter trench (in terrain without timber).

h. Other types. Where tarpaulins, skis, ski poles, or similar items of equipment are available, other types of shelter may be improvised.

Section IV. HEAT

28. Fire Making.

a. Water-resistant matches are items of issue. In order to keep ordinary matches in a usable condition, they should be dipped halfway in heated paraffin and allowed to cool. The paraffin will protect the heads and stick from moisture. Chemical fire-starters may be available and should be saved for emergency use. These are described in TM 3–300.

b. (1) Fires made in snow need bases of green timber (fig. 3). Without such bases, fires will sink into the snow, which melts and extinguishes them. Fire-building material should be carefully prepared in advance. Splinters and shavings obtained from the inside of the split timber should be used to ignite the fire. Inexperienced personnel usually do not secure a sufficient amount of small kindling for starting the fire.

(2) For successful fire building, it is necessary to remember that fire burns upward, and needs air. Large sticks may be arranged in a rectangle as shown in figure 11 ①. The kindling is piled in the center. Small pieces, slightly larger than the kindling splinters, are placed on the kindling paral-

27

lel to one pair of the large base pieces. Another layer is placed at right angles to it, and alternate layers are placed corresponding to the original two until a thickness of about three inches is reached. The pieces can become progressively larger with each layer. Several pieces are placed on the top layer and the kindling ignited.

(3) Another method is to chop small logs into about two-foot lengths; on one side make a series of closely spaced cuts at an angle of about 45°. Make a small tepee with the logs, scored sides faced in, and ignite kindling (fig. 11 ②). This method is not as sure as the first. As the logs burn, additional ones are stacked against the pile. Any plan will succeed which insures plenty of small inflammable kindling to start the fire and enough medium-sized wood to make a bed of coals before the addition of large logs. Candle ends are frequently of value in starting fires.

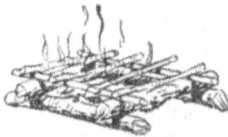

① ②

Figure 11. Fires and fire making.

c. (1) Making fires without matches is most easily accomplished with firearms. Remove the bullet and some powder from the cartridge and loosely place a small oily rag or other tinder in its place. Have kindling prepared for the fire with loose powder on the kindling. Fire the piece into the air, retrieve the rag or tinder, blowing on it to keep it smoldering and apply it to the powder and kindling, blowing until flames appear.

(2) In bright sunlight, fire also may be made without matches by focusing the sun's rays by means of a lens or an improvised lens made of bottle glass.

(3) The best way to produce fire by friction is by bow, thong, drill, press, and tinder board. The process is extremely difficult, even with good equipment.

(4) Chemical firestarters are large and can be lighted even though the hands are stiff. They produce an intense flame and will kindle wet wood.

d. Fires should be small, and should be used by small groups. A small fire allows closer approach than a large one, requires less fuel, melts less snow around it, and is less readily discovered by the enemy.

e. The use of bases and reflectors (fig. 3) magnifies the usable heat of a small fire and should be utilized wherever possible.

f. In extremely cold weather sentries should be designated to keep fires burning in the shelters of men and animals to prevent freezing.

g. Fires and stoves should always be placed in a trench below the level of side benches. The trench should also serve as an entry way. All cold air will then flow to the bottom of the trench and leave the benches remaining at either side comparatively warm from the circulation of heated air over them.

h. Shelters must never be airtight when a fire or lamps are burning inside, as incomplete combustion produces *carbon monoxide*. This is particularly true of shelters with high insulating values, such as snow houses or snow-covered structures.

29. Fuel.

a. OPEN FIRES. (1) The most common form of fuel is wood. Soft wood makes a quick hot fire, but burns out rapidly. Hard wood makes a hot, steady fire. Firewood should be selected from standing dead timber. It should be felled and sawed into proper lengths, and then split. Charcoal makes an excellent fire, since it is smokeless.

(2) In countries with plains, such as the western United States, and certain parts of Canada, China, and Siberia, wood may be almost nonexistent. Substitutes for wood are dried animal dung (buffalo chips) or twisted, coarse grasses and hay.

(3) An oil fire, if it can be protected from the wind, can be made with sand as a wick (*b* below).

b. ENCLOSED FIRES. (1) Gasoline burned in lanterns provides some heat. The one-burner gasoline stove provides great, though localized heat. Candles in inverted tin cans (fig. 12) will take the chill off a small enclosure.

Figure 12. Tin-can candle stove.

(2) Diesel-engine fuel may be used as a substitute in stoves designed to use solid fuel. Fill the bottom of the stove with a layer of sand and provide a constant, slow flow of fuel oil. The sand acts as a wick allowing the oil to burn evenly on the surface.

30. Stoves.

a. The folding Yukon type or the large, standard tent stove may be issued. These are designed for burning wood; however, twisted grass, animal dung (buffalo chips), or fuel oil may be substituted.

b. When stoves are not issued they may be improvised from kerosene, gasoline, milk, coffee, or candy cans.

c. Fireplaces may be contrived in a number of ways. Stone is the best material to use, since it retains heat the longest, and radiates heat long after the fire is extinguished. Stones may also be piled around stoves on three sides; an exceedingly hot fire is maintained in the stove until the stones are heated.

d. In emplacements or dugouts, fireplaces may be cut into the frozen earth of the sides. The life of such a fireplace will be prolonged if it is lined with tin from large cans.

31. Cold Camps.

When, for any reason, it is impossible to have fires in camp or bivouac a few minutes of calisthenics or similar physical exertion will raise the body warmth enough to withstand the chill of undressing in a shelter. Huddling of men together in shelters will raise the temperature. However, crowding sufficient to provide warmth usually creates a heavy concentration of carbon dioxide and vapor, or condensed vapor (frost), from the breathing of the men.

Section V. ESTABLISHMENT OF CAMPS IN EXTREME COLD

32. Selection of Camp Site.

a. Water supply is particularly important in a cold weather camp because of the extreme dehydration of the men after several days' operations in snow, and because the extensive use of dehydrated foods necessitates an unusual amount of water for cooking. Since ice yields more water than snow, the camp should, if possible, be located near a source of ice. Streams are sometimes open even in temperatures as low as 60° below zero; if such a stream is available the camp should be located near it. (See app. I.)

b. Camps should be placed on the downwind side of hills. When practicable they should be placed about halfway or two-thirds up the slope since cold lies at the bottom of valleys.

c. Camps should be placed in timber when possible, as timber affords a good windbreak and, if it is dense, gives some insulation.

d. If in hilly or mountainous terrain, snow on slopes above should be examined to avoid danger from avalanches.

e. The camp should be pitched in the deepest snow available, so that full use of snow insulating properties can be made. Dry powdery snow is the best insulator; compact wet or wind-hardened snow is best for water supply.

f. Camps should be planned in advance. Unit areas, garbage and latrine sites, and command post locations should be designated and marked, and paths taped before construction of the camp begins. Wherever the tactical situation permits, the marking and taping should be done by an advance party.

g. Troops should, if possible, be halted before darkness, and before they are exhausted. Tired troops making camp in darkness and extreme cold neglect measures necessary for their safety; this leads to a gradual reduction in effective personnel strength.

h. Firewood should be located at or near the camp site.

i. While tactical situations may prevent the selection of an ideal camp site, it should possess as many as possible of the above characteristics.

33. One-man Bivouacs.

a. One-man bivouacs will often be necessary because of the value of small unit harassing operations in snow warfare. Although the preparation of such bivouacs is not difficult, individuals should have had cold weather training and experience before they are sent out alone.

b. When the mountain tent is not issued, the snow shelter trench is the most satisfactory form of one-man bivouac.

34. Making Camp.

Upon arrival at the camp site, cooks should immediately begin preparing hot food. Since shelter from the wind and insulation of sleeping equipment are necessary under all conditions of operation in extreme cold, the remaining men are divided into groups and put to work to make the camp habitable.

a. In TIMBER. If it is practicable to use bough for beds (par. 24*a*), a large proportion of the men should be sent to gather them as such beds must be quite thick to be effective. Only lower boughs or isolated trees should be cut, in order to avoid undue reduction of overhead concealment. Groups are detailed to erect the framework of shelters. Other groups supply them with timber. Others wattle and thatch the shelters and bank them with snow. Bough cutting details should bring boughs to a unit distribution point; no boughs should be removed from this point until all men are present and shelters are completed. No one should be permitted to perform detailed work on individual shelters until all shelters are completed. The hot meal should be served, boughs for bedding drawn, and a check of adequacy of all shelters made before dismissal of the men. A standing operating procedure will greatly facilitate the speedy and orderly completion of such work.

b. WITHOUT TIMBER. (1) In open country, snow may be used as described to provide shelter. Often it is better to use tentage and tarpaulins as bedding pads than for their primary purpose, although all cooking should be done in shelter. Since the dispersion necessary to locate units near firewood and bough sources in timber is not necessary in open country, units may be concentrated in snow shelters if the tactical conditions warrant. The concentration of units will insure more efficient use of cooking facilities and will conserve fuel used to thaw snow for water supply. The grouping of men will help to warm the snow shelters by body heat.

(2) Wooden tent pins cannot be driven into frozen ground. Holes for them may be driven with a steel spike, pins inserted in the holes and water poured around them. This is a wasteful method, however, since pins will be broken in attempts to remove them. Iron or steel pins are better. Forty-penny or larger nails make excellent pins for small tents, or rocks may be substituted for pins. The use of pins may be avoided by fastening the guy ropes of tents to poles buried in the snow. Tundra, being moss covered, is suitable for driving wooden pins.

(3) Tents must not be pitched on the down-wind side of large sheltering objects. Snow drifts deeply in such places and is likely to bury the tent-

age. In the woods, this precaution is usually unnecessary.

(4) To provide protection for animals on wind-swept terrain, such as prairie country, canvas shelter should be provided. The animal shelter should be 6 to 6½ feet high, banked around the bottom, and with the entry opening on the downwind side. Horses should be tied on one side of the picket line only. If a heater is used, it should be placed on upwind side inside of the shelter.

35. Sanitation.

a. The necessity for sanitation in camps and bivouacs is not lessened because of cold weather, though cold weather and frozen ground make application of normal sanitary methods difficult. Troops operating in mountains will often find it necessary to procure drinking water by melting snow. Sanitary discipline must be rigidly enforced to prevent indiscriminate pollution of this source of water by human excretion. Large quantities of burlap, neutralizing chemicals, and oil or gasoline, are needed for adequate disposal of wastes during winter. Where transportation permits, large cans may be used as receptacles in latrines. Latrines and garbage dumps may be constructed as shown in figure 13. Hammocks should be made of burlap. Spoil is deposited in the hammocks and collected when frozen.

b. Chemicals such as cresol are spread thickly under the hammocks to neutralize spoil in liquid state. If no chemicals are available, sawdust or shavings should be spread thickly under the hammocks, collected daily, and burned by use of gasoline or oil. Hammocks should be changed daily and burned in a similar manner.

c. If burning is impossible, ground pits should

BURLAP

CHEMICALS

① GARBAGE DISPOSAL

BURLAP

CHEMICALS

② LATRINE

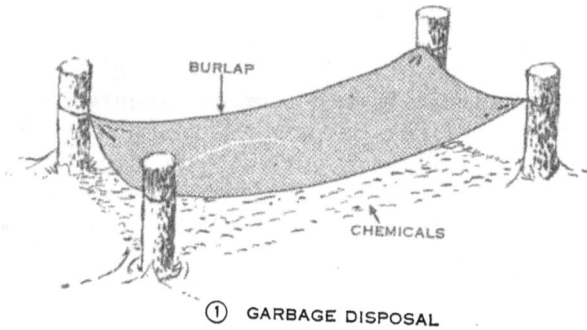

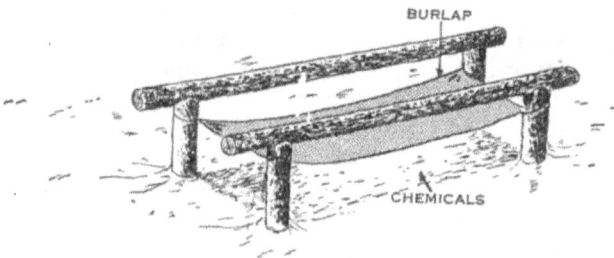

Figure 13. Garbage and latrine hammocks.

be excavated. If the ground is frozen so hard that this is impracticable, snow pits in hollows and valleys not adjacent to water sources should be used, and the site marked and covered with brush. Liberal sprinkling with neutralizing chemicals, if possible, should be effected daily. Spoil should be buried at the first thaw.

d. In cold, windy weather, latrine screens or tents should be erected. Good paths to latrine sites should be cleared. Constant supervision must be exercised to see that all personnel use latrines. If screens or tents are not available, snow holes large enough to protect individuals from the wind should be excavated.

e. Mess gear should be wiped with swabs made of toilet tissue twisted around bough tips before grease and scraps freeze to it. Boiling water should then be used to clean the gear. In addition, germicidal rinse may be used. The use of toilet tissue and boughs will cut down the amount of boiling water needed for cleaning, an important consideration when snow is melted for water supply. Crusted snow may also be used for partial scrubbing of gear. Mess gear should again be dipped in boiling water before subsequent use.

f. Measures for control of lice are of great importance in cold weather because of the difficulty of bathing. Dusting powders should be used as directed by the unit surgeon. Lice are especially apt to be present during a winter campaign where buildings are used as bivouacs. An examination of all personnel for lice infestation before commencement of a winter campaign and frequently thereafter will prevent the spread of lice, particularly if the operations are conducted in a locality where there are no settlements.

g. Shaving in cold weather is difficult but necessary. Growths of beards should be discouraged because faces may freeze under a beard without detection. Moisture from the breath collects in the beard and plays a part in freezing the face. Shaving should be performed at night before retiring. The beard may also be clipped close with hair clippers. These measures will reduce chapping of the skin. Razors and clippers must have the chill removed by heating before being used.

h. Bathing is difficult in extreme cold; however,

bathing as well as laundry facilities should be provided. Dirty clothing and dirty bodies are dangerous in cold weather because dirt destroys the insulating qualities of clothing and dirty skin does not function efficiently in controlling body heat. Steam baths are very good in extreme cold. Steam baths may be improvised in a closed shelter by heating stones and sprinkling water over them. After bathing, a quick snow rub followed by vigorous toweling and dressing in a warm place are ideal. A dry rub is better than nothing at all; feet, crotch, and underarms need particular attention.

36. General Precautions.

a. When conditions permit, camp should be made before dark, security detachments posted, and any available firewood collected at once.

b. Since men are less alert when cold, double sentinels should be posted and relieved at short intervals, often every half hour. Frequent inspection of sentinels by officers and noncommissioned officers will be necessary.

c. In deep snow, paths leading to kitchens, latrines, picket lines, and other places habitually used should be cleared. Necessary paths are also cleared to facilitate movement to, and between, various elements of the outpost.

d. At overnight bivouacs which are not to be occupied later, straddle trenches can be dug in the snow, and when abandoned, covered with brush and marked. Latrines should be protected from the wind by brush, snowbanks, or canvas.

e. For instructions on care of animals see paragraph 68.

f. Snow banked around the lower edge of the tent wall will keep wind from blowing in. Sleeping bags must not be allowed to rest against the tent walls. Insulating material should be used beneath sleeping bags.

g. Cold metal sweats when brought into a warm tent or building. Therefore, firearms are not taken into tents, but are stacked in a secure and orderly manner outside.

h. If there is any frost in the outer layers of clothing, the frosted garments must be removed at once before they thaw. If facilities for thorough drying of garments are not available, it is best to leave them outside and beat the frost out of them immediately, and again before they are put on next morning. Most inner clothing should be removed for drying. Socks and insoles are always damp after a day's march. Under no circumstances should anything be left in the shoes when they are removed. If fires are available, everything should be dried out thoroughly. Care should be taken not to burn the clothing. If fires are not available damp underclothing and socks can be dried by taking them into the sleeping bag. Though the likelihood of arising in the dark in tactical situations may necessitate the wearing of some clothing when in the bag, heavy outside clothing should not be so worn. Wearing frosted clothing in a sleeping bag is a sure way of becoming chilled. It must be remembered that the presence of moisture in any form is the main cause of chilling. Clothing may also be dried by putting it inside clothing near the body while on the move, or still. Sun and wind also help; clothing may be hung in a place where sun and air strike it, or may be hung securely tied to the pack on the march.

i. A heavy fall of damp snow will often break down tents. This can be prevented by having details shake the snow off the tents from time to time.

j. Charcoal burners and incomplete combustion

in gasoline or oil stoves produces monoxide gas poisoning and suffocation in unventilated shelters; for this reason, heated shelters must always be ventilated. Incomplete combustion usually occurs when a top covering touches or is placed down over the flame. ₁

k. Wood or coal stoves must not be placed directly on the snow, otherwise they will soon melt a hole and the fire will be flooded.

l. Care should be taken not to wade in the slush around campfires with shoes that are not waterproof. Frozen feet may be the result.

m. Warming the feet or drying shoes by placing them too close to the fire causes leather to dry and crack. Since leather is tanned skin, it will stand little more heat than a man's hand without damage.

Chapter 5

SNOWSHOES

37. General.

Of the three means of oversnow movement of troops—snowshoe, ski, and oversnow vehicles—the snowshoe will be the most common. For untrained troops the snowshoe is better adapted for normal tactical procedure than the ski. It is also better adapted for use in that type of terrain which provides maximum cover and concealment. Men can pull loads and carry heavy packs better on snowshoes than on skis. Very little special equipment is needed for snowshoe maintenance. For a complete description of issue types of snowshoes, their use, care and maintenance, see TM 10–275.

38. Instruction.

a. Learning to use the snowshoes in marching is not so much a matter of learning a definite technique as it is a matter of continuous use to harden the feet and condition the seldom used muscles that do not come into play in ordinary marching. Two weeks' instruction will usually make troops proficient enough to participate in oversnow operations. Training may be given during the course of operations which are already under way.

b. One period of instruction in the use of snowshoes followed by several periods of extended order drill on snowshoes at quick and double time and a few cross-country marches with packs will prove adequate instruction for snowshoe troops. Stiffness and soreness of muscles can be expected at first; for this reason, initial training should not be too severe. Progressive increase of loads carried and distance covered should be made until full proficiency is reached. Hardening can be accomplished during maneuvers if mobility is of secondary importance.

39. Standards of Proficiency.

Minimum performance should be the ability to carry 50–pounds on a packboard, 10 to 12 miles per day over easy terrain, breaking camp before departure and making camp on arrival. Oversnow vehicles, when available, should be used for trail breaking. Since trail breaking by man power is fatiguing work, trail breakers should be changed at frequent intervals. It is important that men have sufficient reserve energy for bivouac construction at the end of a march.

40. Use of Snowshoes.

a. GENERAL. Snowshoes should always be worn when snow is more than 12 inches deep; they should not be worn when it is less than 3 inches deep. In shallow snow, the webbing of snowshoes will be damaged by rocks, sticks, and clods and mobility on foot is greater without snowshoes. Except in shallow snow, snowshoes are suitable for use in all but the densest wooded and brush areas. The bearpaw type is suitable for use around crew-served weapons and animals, or in very rough or steep terrain.

b. SOFT SNOW OR BREAKABLE CRUST. (1) In soft snow or snow with a breakable crust, a trail snowshoe should be worn, as a man wearing a bearpaw snowshoe sinks in quite a distance, sometimes to the knee.

(2) To conserve energy and to cover a maximum distance, a long stride is best. The development of the proper stride requires a considerable amount of training. The foot is lifted straight up and then

42

thrust forward. Before lifting the foot, it is pulled backwards an inch or so before stepping ahead. This frees the tip of the snowshoe and enables it to clear the snow on the forward movement.

c. HARD OR PACKED SNOW. In hard or packed snow, a shorter stride is more effective. Because the hard snow supports the foot, the spring-like tension on the webbing is lost and a long "heel and toe" stride is very hard on the knees. The fastest and least fatiguing method of traveling is to use a loose-kneed, rocking gait.

d. RUGGED TERRAIN. After a man has learned to use snowshoes on level land, he should be advanced to practice in negotiating rugged terrain. A steep hill can be traversed with trail shoes. The shoe is not turned flat against the slope of the hill, but a trail is beaten down by stamping the inner shoe at each step and by placing as little weight as possible on the outer one. However, care should be taken to avoid cutting a trail across an avalanche slope. While a snowshoe trail is less likely to start an avalanche than a ski trail, a snowshoe party is on the slope for a longer period due to the difficulty of making the traverse. On crusted or packed snow, the slope can best be climbed direct. When traversing on hard snow the snowshoe will necessarily be placed flat on the surface but the toe should point diagonally up hill for better application of friction. When the crust is strong enough, it is often profitable to remove the snowshoes on a traverse. The spikes on the bear-paw snowshoe permit climbing any degree of slope that can be climbed without step cutting.

e. OBSTACLES. Logs, ditches and small streams can be jumped. Care should be taken to prevent the tail of the snowshoe from falling downward. If the tail is in a vertical position upon landing, it will

43

strike the snow first and perhaps throw the user.

f. TURNING ABOUT. To turn about on a trail, a kick turn is used. The right leg is lifted, swung back and kicked forward and up. At the top of the kick, as the trailing edge of the snowshoe clears the snow, the foot is turned outward, the turning of the foot continuing as the leg is lowered, when it will be 180° opposed to its original facing. The weight is gradually shifted to the right foot as it is lowered, until the left foot can be raised and brought over the trailing edge of the right snowshoe, now at rest on the snow, and faced in the direction of the right foot.

Chapter 6

SKIING

41. General.

a. Trained ski troops have a high degree of over-snow mobility, and are capable of brilliant and daring small unit actions. Scouts and reconnaissance units should be accomplished ski troops whenever possible. A good portion of the infantry components should be capable of using skis, if necessary. Ski troops are also suited for special missions against enemy supply points and columns.

b. For a description of issue types of skis, their use, care, and maintenance, see TM 10–275.

42. Training.

a. Units engaged in ski training should have completed unit and combined training.

b. Training highly proficient skiers for such duties as reconnaissance, carrying messages, and patrolling in the mountains, is a lengthy process. The training period can be shortened considerably if men with previous training are utilized.

c. Training should begin with physical training to include ski conditioning exercises, followed in order by elementary skiing, cross-country skiing, and advanced technique. Only limited instruction in downhill skiing should be given until extended cross-country marches with full military equipment on level or rolling terrain have been accomplished. Roads and trails should be avoided whenever possible. Since hill climbing ability is important, this phase of training should be emphasized. At the conclusion of training, the soldier should be able to travel safely with a pack and as a member of a unit, over all sorts of rugged, snow-covered terrain.

d. For additional information on skiing, see appendix II.

Chapter 7
OVERSNOW VEHICLES

Section I. GENERAL
43. General.

The use of oversnow vehicles enables transport to be independent of roads and to operate across country, and turns snow-covered terrain into an asset rather than a liability. Motorized oversnow vehicles should be characterized by an extremely low track or runner pressure, high power, durability, and ease of maintenance. Wheeled-vehicle transportation becomes useless in deep snow and, as road clearance is not possible in forward areas and as the road net may be sparse, or even non-existent, the substitution of oversnow vehicles for wheeled vehicles in forward areas is imperative. Oversnow vehicles should augment wheeled transport in rear areas during winter months. Most track-laying types of oversnow vehicles are suitable for cross-country operation all year round and in all weather.

44. Types.

Oversnow vehicles are usually track laying or runner borne. Track-laying types are usually slower than runner-borne, but capable of heavier duty. Runner-borne types may be best utilized in damp snow and open, smooth, or rolling terrain, while track-laying types are best for rough terrain. The powdery nature of snow in extreme cold necessitates greater flotation than that required in ordinary snow.

45. Load Factors.

a. The variables of load, terrain, vegetation, and condition and depth of the snow modify performance of all oversnow vehicles. Loads should be as light as possible, clear routes should be selected by liaison aircraft, and towed sleds or toboggans should be narrower than the towing vehicles.

b. Speed of operation should be kept as low as consistent with the tactical situation if excessive mortality of vehicles is to be prevented.

c. Oversnow vehicles designed for reconnaissance and rapid oversnow movement should not be used to haul loads. Medium load-pulling or carrying equipment should never be substituted for heavy tractors.

Section II. OVERSNOW MOTORIZED VEHICLES

46. Types.

There are several types of oversnow motorized vehicles. One standard type is illustrated in figure 14.

Figure 14. Cargo carrier M29.

47. Motor Winterization.

For winterization of vehicles, see section II, chapter 10 and the winterization sections of appropriate technical publications.

48. Track Adjustment.

Extreme cold contracts metals and makes rubber brittle. Tracks should be adjusted in the temperature in which they are to be used. A track which is tight in a warm garage will break easily after being in a temperature of 40° below zero for a short time.

49. Care.

Track-laying oversnow vehicles are not tanks, and should never be used to crush obstacles. Engines should not be raced nor tracks spun. Route reconnaissance should be thorough; drivers must be on the alert to select routes which will save wear on their vehicles. Care of runners on runner-borne oversnow equipment is the same as for sleds. Runner-borne equipment should not be operated at high speeds unless it is known that the snow is uniform throughout the route, and that the route is free from obtacles.

50. Driver Training.

a. Drivers should be trained in basic driving, maneuvers, hill climbing, towing loads, selecting routes, freeing bogged vehicles, replacing tracks, first echelon maintenance, and, when time and facilities permits, second echelon maintenance. The training should be concluded with a series of practical tests.

b. Drivers are taught to avoid obstructions of all kinds, rather than to rely on the characteristics of the vehicles in overcoming such obstacles. *Racing of engines is to be avoided,* as this is a particularly injurious practice at low temperature. Each driver should be carefully checked for proficiency in operating the type of vehicle which is to be assigned to him. Once so assigned, the vehicle should remain in his care and under his operation.

51. First and Second Echelon Maintenance.

First and second echelon maintenance are more important in extreme cold than under normal conditions. Proper driving technique and engine care

are absolutely essential to prevent early ruin of motors in cold weather. Proficiency in winterization of vehicles should be stressed. Technical publications applying to the type of oversnow vehicles issued should be on hand and carefully adhered to, as mechanical failure is likely and the resupply of parts is difficult.

Section III. NONMOTORIZED VEHICLES
52. General.

a. The availability of manpower and possible shortage of motorized oversnow equipment may require the use of man-drawn sleds and toboggans for transport of supplies for short distances.

b. Men hauling loads should work on foot if the snow depth is less than 12 inches and on snowshoes if it is over 12 inches.

c. Tandem harnessing is necessary when off roads. With this type of harnessing the energy of only one man is dissipated in breaking the trail. The harness should be of hip harness type. On roads other types of harness may prove advantageous.

d. The employment of one man behind a sled, using handlebars for pushing and steering, and a rope for braking the sled is of great advantage, even though the pulling team is thereby diminished in size. In rounding curves, all men in harness swing wide to the outside of the curve to prevent the teams and sled from slipping off the road to the inside. Skis, unless equipped with skins, do not possess sufficient traction to be used in hauling.

53. Sleds and Toboggans.

a. COMBINATION SLED-TOBOGGAN (fig. 15). This sled is standard and is the type most likely to be issued for operations in snow and cold. It can be used as a sled when the snow offers a firm bearing surface or the load is light. It can be used as a toboggan when the snow is light and powdery, or when the load is heavy.

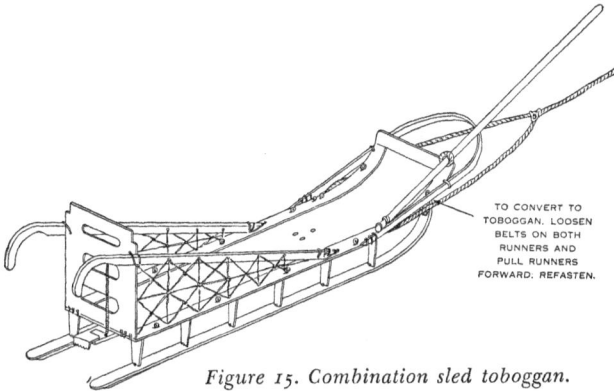

TO CONVERT TO TOBOGGAN, LOOSEN BELTS ON BOTH RUNNERS AND PULL RUNNERS FORWARD, REFASTEN.

Figure 15. Combination sled toboggan.

b. Standard Military Toboggan (fig. 16). This toboggan can be tractor drawn or man hauled.

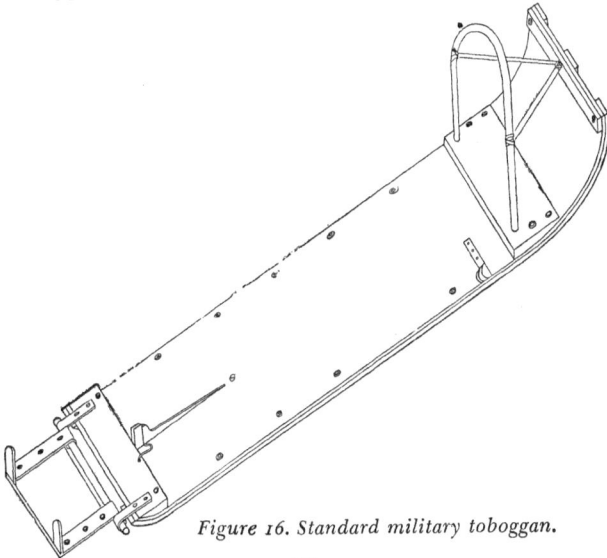

Figure 16. Standard military toboggan.

c. AKJA (figs. 17, 18, 19). The akja may be used for the removal of wounded from the firing line and for transport of supplies to forward units. For short distances (approximately 200 to 300 yards) it can be pulled by one man crawling or creeping. It can readily be improvised from plywood paneling, as shown in figure 18.

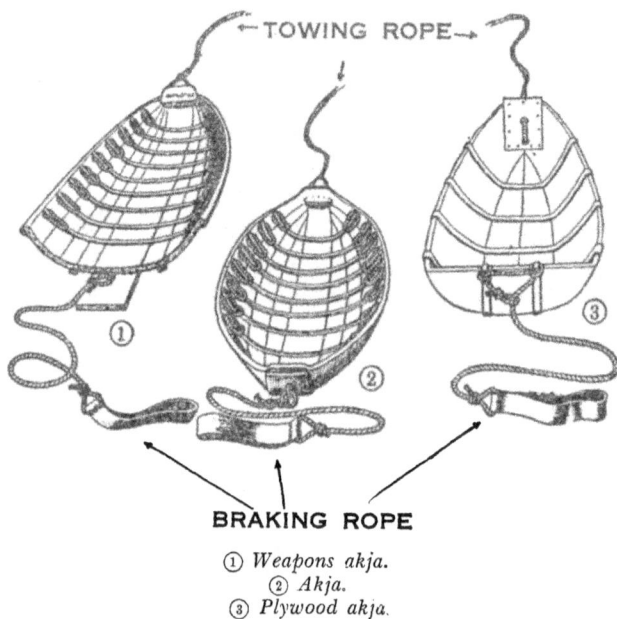

① *Weapons akja.*
② *Akja.*
③ *Plywood akja.*

Figure 17. Akja sleds.

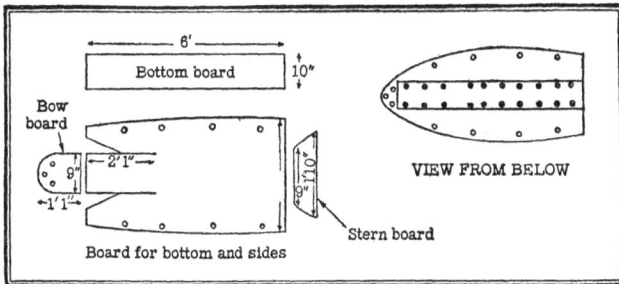

Figure 18. Construction of plywood akja.

METHOD OF LOOPING TOWROPE
FOR CRAWLING OR CREEPING

Figure 19. Use of akja in combat.

d. TRACTOR-DRAWN CARGO SLED (fig. 20). Tractor-drawn cargo sleds are capable of carrying loads
up to 1,400 pounds. Figures show the standard
cargo sled fitted with wooden adapters carrying the
105–mm howitzer broken into separate loads and
being drawn by an M29 cargo carrier. The trail
should be broken by one unloaded cargo carrier
when cargo sleds are heavily loaded. Slopes up to
20 percent have been negotiated by use of this
equipment. The prime mover should always be
wider than any sled or toboggan.

53

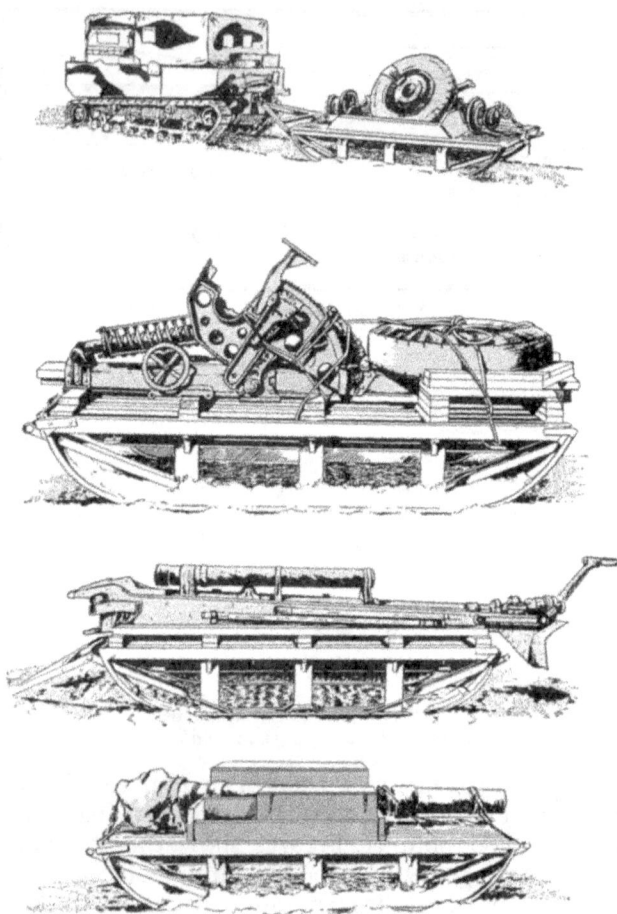

Figure 20. Cargo sleds loaded with 105-mm. howitzer, knocked-down. One sled drawn by cargo carrier M29.

e. Other types of sleds or toboggans may be available.

54. Improvised Sleds and Toboggans.

a. When improvising sleds, the runners must be of such size as to support the sled and its load a sufficient distance above the snow surface to prevent the body of the sled from touching the surface. The runners must be turned up enough to prevent burying or plowing of the front end. It is usually simpler to adjust the load to the sled than to attempt to build the sled to fit the load. A sled may be improvised from skis and ski poles as well as from lumber. (See fig. 21.)

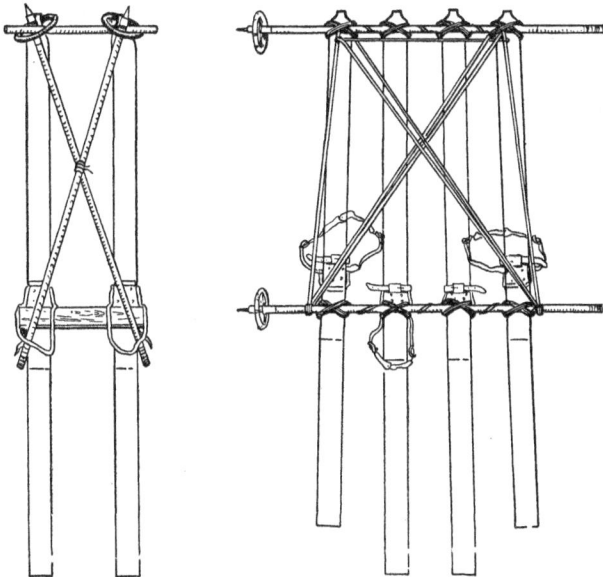

Figure 21. Sled improvised from ski equipment.

b. Toboggans may be most easily improvised from sheet metal, although combinations of wood and sheet metal are lighter. The sheet metal should be used for the curved portion only. The standard toboggan may be used as a guide for improvisation.

c. A travois, or drag, may be used for light loads. It is readily constructed as shown in figure 22.

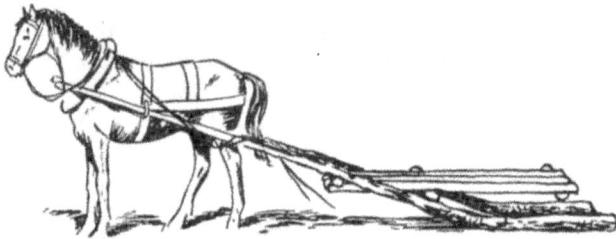

Figure 22. Travois or drag.

d. Sliding troughs (fig. 23) are effective for transportation of heavy weapons; one trough is placed under each wheel. A trough is constructed of planks, preferably ash, placed side by side. Planks should be steamed and bent over a form while hot. Bearing surfaces should be waxed. (See par. 55.) Approximate load capacities for troughs of various sizes are as follows:

Load Capacity Table for One Trough

Load	Length	Width
Pounds	*Feet*	*Inches*
330	7½	13
660	12	16
1750	17	19

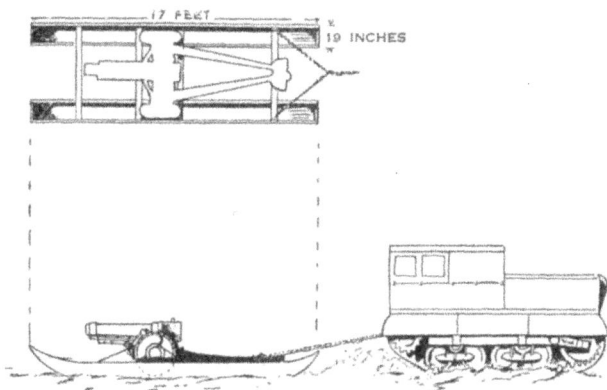

Figure 23. 105-mm howitzer drawn in troughs.

55. Adjustment of Bearing Surfaces.

Bearing surfaces of sleds, troughs and toboggans require waxing to suit snow conditions. (See sec. IV, app. II.) At extremely low temperatures snow offers almost as much friction to sliding as sand; at such temperatures waxes are no longer efficient. Metal or metal shod runners may be covered with wood when snow begins to impede progress. Wooden runners and toboggans may be iced at low temperatures by pouring water over the bearing surfaces; their subsequent freezing is an effective expedient. Sleds and toboggans will freeze to the snow surface if left standing in one spot loaded. They may be broken out by tapping runners steadily with a mallet or stick of wood, and then moving the sled. Toboggans are more difficult to break out, and snow frozen to the bottom will make them hard to pull until friction removes it.

56. Adjustment of Combination Sled-Toboggans.

a. When loads are light and snow is compacted,

57

crusted or wet, the combination sled toboggan should be employed as a sled, since its frictional resistance is less in this position; in addition, with the load remaining constant, greater speed is possible as a sled than as a toboggan.

b. With soft powdery snow, a weak crust, wet slush, or heavy loads, sled runners bury themselves, and the sled will plow through, rather than glide over, the snow. When these conditions exist it will be necessary to adjust the combination sled-toboggan to form a toboggan. As a toboggan the pressure per unit area of bearing surface is less than the sled will not bury nor plow.

57. Tarpaulins.

Tarpaulins used to cover loads become stiff in extreme cold. They should not be sharply creased when stiff or the threads will break; they will also wear out quickly if continually creased at the same point.

58. Loads.

a. Wood becomes very brittle in extreme cold. Furthermore, concentration of the load over the front or rear portions of a sled reduces the elasticity of the runner at that point. Hence, unless the load is centered on the sled the danger of breaking runners is increased. Centering of loads is best accomplished by placing heavy articles, particularly those whose weight is concentrated, slightly to the rear of the center of the sled and loading lighter articles on top and at either end. This makes the sled easier to steer than when the load is exactly centered. Overloading should be avoided since a small amount of additional strain on runners whose elasticity has been impaired by cold is sufficient to break them.

b. Loads should be placed low upon the sled. Certain items comprising the load—bedding rolls, sleeping bags, and tentage—may be compacted and wedged firmly in the sled. The load is then completely covered by a tarpaulin and lashed to the sled. Equipment likely to be needed on the trail should be stowed in waterproof bags and lashed on the load outside of the tarpaulin. Lashings should permit no movement between load and sled in any direction. After traveling awhile, it will again be necessary to tighten the lashings.

59. Lashings.

a. The beds of sleds and toboggans should have a row of loops of rope or metal eyes through which lashings may be passed. A good method is to make these loops long, yet not long enough to meet when the load is compacted and covered. A center rope is tied to a loop or eye at the stern and tied loosely on the bow. Lashings are tied to the rear loop on either side and passed alternately around the center rope and through loops as shown until they are fastened to the bow. These lashings, one on either side, hold the load in place and should be drawn taut. In order to permit later adjustment, the center rope is not taught originally. The center rope should be pulled taught after the load has settled. (See fig. 24.)

b. Cotton or linen rope is more pliable and retains more strength at low temperatures than that made from hemp or sisal and is therefore superior to the latter as lashing material.

c. Lashings should be padded at points of chafing, since a sled is flexible and the constant moving of a lashing over a sharp or rough surface will wear it out.

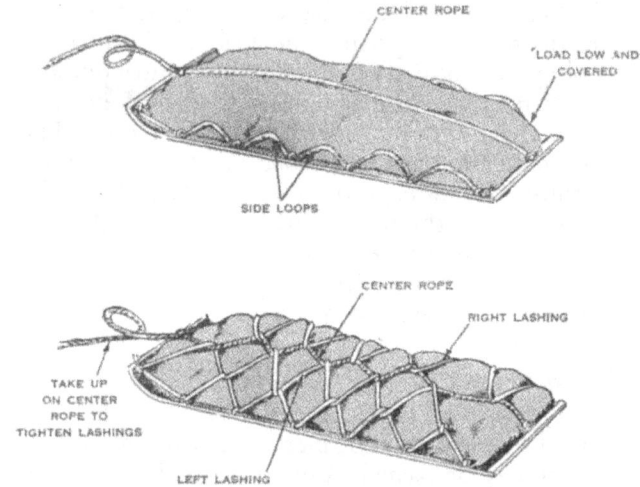

Figure 24. Loop, lashings, and their equipment.

d. Lashings and other ropes should be coiled when not in use, as abrupt kinks at low temperatures break the threads.

60. Maintenance and Field Repair.

a. SLEDS. The breaking of runners is the most common form of damage to sleds. When a runner breaks, the edges of the break should be matched together. A block is then nailed or screwed on top of the runner covering the joint. A ski can then be fastened to the running surface of the runner.

b. TOBOGGANS. Holes in toboggans may be mended by nailing a flattened can on the under side of the toboggan and covering the hole. A ski is frequently fastened over the mended point to reinforce it.

c. MATERIALS. Nails, bolts, tacks, screws, hammers, wrenches, screw-drivers, and rawhide thongs should be kept in a small bag fastened to each sled or toboggan for ready use in localities where damage to oversnow equipment is most likely to occur.

61. Time and Space Factors.

a. GENERAL. Because of the variables affecting oversnow movement, rates of travel are difficult to determine. Packed or crusted snow on level ground free from brush, stumps or rocks, and with a medium load at zero temperature, is ideal for oversnow movement. The delay caused by the darkness, when traveling at night, is frequently compensated for by the presence of a firm crust of snow which may be absent in the daytime because of the solar thawing which occurs even at low air temperatures.

b. AVERAGE DAILY RUN. (1) The length of the daily run depends on many variable factors, such as the use of power and manhauling, stops for drying, establishment of bivouacs along the route, supply difficulties, and delays incident to river crossings. The use of light equipment will increase the length of the run; the use of heavier equipment correspondingly decreases it.

(2) For oversnow marches across terrain lacking shelter and road nets, many unscheduled halts will occur. Failure to halt for drying will result in early incapacitation of the command. The daily run can be increased by the use of winter-trained engineers to keep the routes in good condition, proper cargo sleds and other oversnow vehicles, extensive use of liaison aircraft for route reconnaissance, and the elimination of all but essential equipment.

c. LOADS. (1) For the combination sled-toboggan drawn by four men and steered by one man 300 pounds is the load recommended for operational use. This figure is for loose powdery snow;

the load will vary under different snow conditions. These loads can be increased on a well broken trail or on good snow.

(2) One man can pull 200 pounds in an akja for short distances. For long distances a one-man sled load should not exceed 75 pounds.

d. SPEED. Speed of hauling by sled is less than that of packing by packboard. To obtain speed, men must be hardened to pulling by progressively increasing loads and distances until maximum performance is obtained.

Chapter 8

ANIMAL TRANSPORT

Section I. GENERAL

62. Limitations.

Animal transport is not recommended because animals must be fed whether working or not and the transportation of their food, bulkier than engine fuel, will overload supply facilities already strained by increased demands. Animals, particularly mules, suffer from cold and require correspondingly more attention than motors, and are often noisy. Horse-drawn and mule-drawn vehicles on wheels are moved with difficulty over roads when the snow is as much as a foot deep. During subzero temperatures, wheeled vehicles are harder to pull through snow than when the weather is warmer. (See FM 25-5.) Deep snow prevents the use of heavy draft animals. At times, the lack of motorized equipment and the availability of animals and their food will outweigh these general objections. Under these conditions, native animals are preferable since they are hardened to the local climate.

Section II. TYPES OF ANIMALS, USES, AND EQUIPMENT

63. Horses and Mules.

A snow depth of 1 foot or less permits the use of horses and mules. They can be used as pack animals or as draft animals for sleds, toboggans or travois. Heavier loads can be drawn on sleds than can be carried by packs.

64. Reindeer.

a. Reindeer are found in arctic regions of North America, Europe, and parts of Asia. Chiefly because of their availability, they should be used if operations in these regions occur. Their use away from their natural habitat should not be considered as their care and equipment are specialized, and their limited possibilities preclude the training of handlers; this last condition necessitates the hiring of natives accustomed to the use of reindeer. The reindeer is a sturdy draft animal and requires less attention in cold than does a horse.

b. Reindeer can be used to draw light sleds and travois.

65. Camels.

In Central Asia, the Bactrian camel is used as a cold weather draft or pack animal. If the camel is available, it should be used with native handlers and equipment.

66. Dogs.

a. Dogs are best used for hauling operations on a fixed route between established supply points at which dog food has been placed. This obviates the necessity for carrying more than a small supply of dog food, and permits a corresponding increase in the amount of other supplies carried.

b. In addition to their hauling power, dogs are also very valuable as aids to sentinels in cold weather operation. The winter hours of darkness are long, the cold induces lethargy in sentinels, and dogs can detect an enemy force before a man can do so. Dogs may also be used as scout dogs and messenger dogs. For further details, see FM 25–6.

c. Skiers may use dogs to assist in hauling sleds. When using well-trained dogs, the skier may precede them to break trail.

67. Horses and Mules as Pack Animals.

a. Horses and mules can carry packs in deep snow easier than they can draw sleds. Horses serve better in snow than mules, because the latter, with their small hoofs, sink into the snow more readily.

b. The length of the day's march for pack animals depends on many variable factors. With no other pay load, a pack animal can carry approximately 10 days' forage supply for one animal.

c. When the standard pack saddle is not available, a light pack for horse or mule may be improvised as shown in figure 25.

Figure 25. Improvised light horse pack.

Section III. CARE AND MANAGEMENT

68. Horses and Mules.

a. SHELTER AND BEDDING. Cold weather shelters with fires and bedding must be provided for horses and mules. Blankets should also be provided and should be kept clean and dry. Bedding should be thick; if the shelter is not heated, sentinels should examine animals periodically to see that they do not freeze. Unless adequate bedding is available, animals must not be permitted to sleep lying down during extremely cold weather.

b. CARE IN WATERING AND FEEDING. (1) Water and feed should, if possible, be warmed before consumption.

(2) Frequently normal watering methods are inadequate or unsuitable in cold weather. Holes cut into the ice on streams or lakes provide practicable water troughs from which animals can drink without difficulty. Holes should be about 18 to 24 inches square at the top, and shaped like an inverted truncated pyramid about 6 inches square at the bottom. The basin thus cut will fill with water, especially as the animals approach the edge. The edges should be roughened for a distance of about 2 feet to provide better footing to prevent the animals from slipping into the hole.

(3) To prevent warm animals from drinking too fast, bits should be left in their mouths, or straw, twigs, leaves, etc. should be thrown into the water.

c. CARE WHILE WORKING. (1) Horses and mules should not be forced to exert themselves in temperatures lower than 20° below zero because, in such temperatures, deep breathing from exertion subjects them to frosted lungs. Balls of ice often form in their nostrils and prevent breathing. Both of these conditions can be avoided to some extent by the use of nostril shields of burlap sacking made to fit loosely around the animal's muzzle and having an open end hanging about 6 inches below the nose. Bits should be warmed before use, and should be cloth or tape covered.

(2) Animals operating over ice, or snow and ice, should be rough shod to prevent slipping. Hoofs should be inspected frequently and caked snow removed from the soles. In snow, animals without shoes will operate with less difficulty. Hooves do not pack with snow and the footing afforded is adequate. Burlap padding for hoofs may also be necessary at extreme temperatures.

(3) On long steep pulls, half of the vehicles should be pulled to the top with double teams, all teams then being sent back to pull up the remaining vehicles in similar fashion. In this connection, it is well to remember that sleds are more easily drawn through snow than are wheeled vehicles. It is therefore advantageous to place runners under the wheels of wheeled vehicles.

d. CARE AFTER WORKING. Animals should be given frequent rests; at such times sweaty patches under the harness should be wiped dry. When animals are unhitched or unsaddled they should be wiped dry, blanketed, led until they have cooled off, and (if possible) protected from the wind. They should never be watered when they are hot, since overheated animals drinking large quantities of cold water are apt to founder.

69. Reindeer, Camels and Dogs.

The care and management of reindeer and camels should be left to native drivers and handlers. (See pars. 64 and 65.) The care and management of dogs is covered in FM 25–6.

Chapter 9

EQUIPMENT

Section I. PACKS

70. General.

a. A good pack for operations in extreme cold should be capable of carrying 60 pounds or more in weight, and must be loose enough to prevent constriction of the arms and to allow air to circulate between the pack and the wearer's back to permit evaporation of perspiration. The packboard meets all of these requirements; the rucksack meets all except the weight carrying ability, but has the advantage for skiers of having a low center of gravity. Ordinarily, a low center of gravity is highly undesirable; however, it is necessary for skiing. Standard field packs are unsatisfactory for cold weather use, partly because of their limited capacity and partly because they allow no ventilation beneath the pack.

b. For a complete discussion of the construction, use, and care of rucksacks and packboards, see TM 10–275.

Section II. RUCKSACKS

71. General.

The purpose of the rucksack is to provide a pack capable of carrying necessities for a ski trooper or mountain climber for a short trip away from his base. When loaded as designed, the weight will be concentrated low and next to the frame. The normal load for a rucksack is 40 pounds. Overloading causes undue strain on the wearer, since a considerable amount of his effort must be expended in preventing the rucksack from pulling him over backward. The low center of gravity, with considerable weight resting on the hips, is desirable for men actually climbing steep slopes or skiing, but is undesirable for hiking where the weight must be kept high on the shoulders to avoid exhaustion. When lightly and properly loaded, the rucksack is the most suitable pack for the ski trooper and mountaineer. Bulky loads, even if light, tend to destroy the balance of the rucksack. The necessity for a ski trooper or mountaineer to keep his center of gravity low dictates the use of the rucksack by such troops. However, it should not be used by troops who habitually march on foot or snowshoes.

72. Packing.
In packing the rucksack, the weight should be concentrated in the lower forward portion of the sack and the pack kept thin from front to rear. The back of the rucksack should slant forward.

73. Use with Packboard.
The rucksack removed from its frame can be used as one component of the load of a packboard. Usually it is fastened about midway up on the packboard and a parka and tentage are rolled and fastened above it.

Section III. PACKBOARDS
74. Characteristics.
Packboards have a greater weight-carrying ability than any other kind of pack, and allow the carrying of heavy loads or irregular shapes without discomfort to the wearer. Adapters and quick release straps are also issued with packboards to make them suitable for transport of heavy weapons and ammunition.

75. Standard Packboard.

The standard packboard is the plywood type. It is made of a rectangular back molded into a curved edge about 2 inches deep on either side. Canvas is stretched tightly across from one edge to the other to keep the board away from the body of the wearer. Sections are cut out of the back to save weight; metal hooks are fastened to either side to provide anchorage for lashings. The board is quite sturdy, but should not be subjected to twisting strains because of its laminated construction. The canvas backing should be kept clean and tight; the board should never be thrown to the ground when loaded but should, instead, be lowered gently. The hooks should not be bent. The board is loaded by lashing a field pack, rucksack (less frame), duffle bag, or barracks bag to the back and, if necessary, by lashing tentage and sleeping bag (in waterproof or water repellent roll) horizontally across the top. Weight should be kept high on the board, and load kept thin from front to back. (See fig. 26.)

Figure 26. Plywood packboard.

76. Special Types.

There are many special types of packboards, but most of them require experienced personnel to get the best results. Army personnel using packboards will not ordinarily have the requisite experience to get such results, and the necessity for intensive training in other phases of cold weather living and operations will preclude any great length of time being devoted to training in their use.

77. Packing.

Carrying loads of equipment and supplies by packboard is faster and better suited to rough terrain and deep powdery snow than man-hauling by sleds, but necessitates more frequent trips because of the lighter loads carried. Man-hauling by sleds is preferable on flat terrain under favorable conditions. If the supplies and equipment can be broken down into loads whose bulk and weight are suited to packing, it is usually the better method of man transport, not being as fatiguing as hauling. Packboards are well suited to marching troops or troops on snowshoes, but are unsuitable for ski troops because their high center of gravity makes balance while skiing difficult.

Section IV. SLEEPING EQUIPMENT

78. General.

For a discussion of various types of sleeping equipment, their care and use, see TM 10-275.

79. Insulation.

Sleeping equipment must always be insulated from the snow, not only to provide comfort to the sleeper but also to protect the bag against wetting due to melting of the snow by body heat in shelters. Soft articles of clothing should be laid smoothly under the bottom of the sleeping bag, between the bag and cover, to act as an insulating mattress for the sleeper. Snow should be brushed carefully from the surface of the bag and cover before packing. The sleeping bag should be dried at every opportunity, as a bag which is continually damp will eventually lose a part or all of its insulating value.

80. Improvised Sleeping Bag.

If sleeping bags are not available, substitute bags may be made from shelter halves and blankets, and extra clothing used for sleeping pads.

81. Immediate Availability.

Unavoidable and long delays of unit kitchen and baggage trains will occur frequently when operating in extreme cold weather areas. For this reason sleeping equipment should be carried by each individual.

Section V. MISCELLANEOUS EQUIPMENT

82. Insulating Pad.

The insulating pad is a necessity when operating in nonwooded areas of extreme cold. It is also convenient in wooded areas, in that its use enables the individual to use fewer boughs, with a consequent saving of time and effort. It may be conveniently placed in a rucksack. To place it in the rucksack, loosen the rucksack drawstring, bend the pad in a U shape and insert it in the open rucksack, the open portion of the U toward the front. Press on the pad so that its shape conforms to that of the rucksack. It is bent around the curved back portion of the sack with its longitudinal axis horizontal.

83. Snow Goggles.
Sunlight in snowy areas, especially when diffused by haze or clouds, can seriously injure the eyes. Goggles prevent snowblindness and improve vision in unbroken snow and sunlight.

84. Mountain Brush.
The mountain brush has a value in operations in snow out of proportion to its small size. Frequent brushing of snow from clothing and equipment prevents accumulation of moisture from melting snow. Every individual should have one of these brushes in his possession.

85. Extra Tent Ropes.
Extra tent ropes are invaluable for the construction of shelters, for use as drying racks, and for tying or lashing improvised equipment. They are valuable for supplementing or replacing lashings and bindings of all kinds.

86. Machetes.
A machete or bolo is useful in operations in wooded terrain for trimming boughs, felling small trees, and clearing brush.

87. Hatchets, Axes, Saws.
This equipment is necessary in wooded terrain for the procurement of firewood, building material, and bedding.

88. Combat Knife.
In addition to its use in combat, the combat knife has many other uses in cold weather bivouacs. It is used to prepare fuel for fires and to fashion im-

provised equipment. It is also used for preparing and cooking food as well as in eating it.

89. Tent Stoves.
Some large tent stoves are necessary to provide drying facilities to units rotated to the reserve. The heat from large stoves quickly dries equipment and clothing; the use of such stoves in shelters is necessary if fighting efficiency is to be maintained.

90. Wannigans and Houses.
A wannigan is a small movable house, usually on large runners. Wannigans can be used as operating rooms, command posts, and similar installations. If prefabricated houses are not available, wannigans may be improvised by building light frameworks, covered with tarpaper, on the drag or runners.

91. Availability of Equipment.
When planning an operation in a cold area, specialized equipment suitable to the area should be obtained and proper instruction in its use given to all members of the command by persons competent to do so. The type of cold, whether wet or dry, should be anticipated, as the requirements for the two extremes vary so widely as to be almost opposite. Specialized equipment may not be available to commanders who, through premature onset of winter or enemy pressure, are forced to operate in snow and cold. In these cases, the use of expedients should be resorted to. However, expedients can never replace anticipation and proper planning, and a commander forced to resort to their use will be operating at a disadvantage.

92. Expedients.
Some expedients which will help to preserve the

health and comfort of inadequately equipped troops operating in extreme cold, are as follows:

a. Insoles may be improvised from blankets, burlap sacking, dried and shredded grass, moss, or paper. Overshoes of the cloth-topped variety used with insoles and extra socks and foot wrappings cut from blankets will serve as substitutes for mukluks. Regular shoes should not be worn inside the overshoes; the extra space may be filled with addi- ·ional socks, foot wrappings, hay, straw, grass or dry moss.

b. Mufflers and face shields may be improvised from old blankets.

c. Snow goggles may be improvised by cutting slits in a piece of wood covering the eyes. A piece of leather having small holes cut for eyeholes is effective. Lampblack rubbed around the eyes affords some protection against glare.

d. Drying racks may be constructed in shelters by the use of tent ropes, wooden racks, or wooden poles covered by chicken wire. They should be placed at the highest point of the shelter, so that the warm air will better dry the equipment they support.

e. Packboards may be quickly improvised by the construction of light wooden frames, with target cloth or other cloth sewed over them and doped with airplane dope. Screws may be fastened into the sides for lashings.

f. Beds may be insulated by paper, or flattened pasteboard ammunition containers or ration boxes.

Chapter 10
SPECIAL CARE OF WEAPONS AND EQUIPMENT

Section I. GENERAL
93. General.

At temperatures consistently below 0° difficulties such as those enumerated in paragraph 2d are encountered in the care of weapons and equipment. Extremely careful servicing by both operating and maintenance personnel is required, if poor performance and total functional failure are to be avoided. For detailed description of the procedure to be followed in overcoming such difficulties, refer to the appropriate technical manual. Descriptions of certain general procedures are contained in paragraphs which follow.

94. Range of Low Temperatures.

Most equipment will function satisfactorily down to 20° below zero with lubricants and preservatives prescribed for +32° to 0°. Below that temperature all matériel requires winterization. Special precautions must be taken. Temperatures of 20° to 60° below zero are the temperatures considered for the expression "extreme cold" in this manual. Temperatures of 60° to 90° below zero, though common to some localities, are relatively infrequent. A considerable portion of the land area of the world is subject to temperatures varying from 20° to 60° below zero.

95. Condensation.

a. When there is an abrupt change in the relative temperatures of the air and a metallic or glass object with which it is in contact, the warm air is chilled, causing the moisture from the air to deposit or condense on the cold matériel. In general, this applies to cold matériel, such as a rifle or telescope, brought indoors, and results in condensation on the exposed surfaces. However, if equipment with internal air spaces is assembled at warm temperatures and then moved outdoors, condensation will occur inside the air space. Condensation is objectionable because of its injurious effects. If not wiped off, it causes rust and corrosion; or when moved outdoors later it freezes, sometime making mechanisms inoperative. It also renders glass opaque, leads to the presence of water in closed containers such as fuel drums, and produces an undesirable emulsion with lubricants. Condensation may be prevented by keeping arms, ammunition and equipment at the same temperature as the air in which it is to be operated.

b. Unheated anterooms or porches should be used for storing weapons of men living in heated shelters. Muzzle and breech covers should be installed on the weapons and kept securely fastened, to prevent the wind from driving snow under the covers. Bores should be cleaned frequently; if ice has formed, hot oil may be used to melt it for removal before cleaning. After firing, weapons should be cleaned while still warm. For large caliber weapons, use warm water if available to make the standard soda ash solution. If the gun has become cold, treat the soda solution with alcohol, glycerine or antifreeze compound, as indicated in the appropriate Technical Manual, to prevent freezing. Clean small arms bores while still warm with rifle bore cleaner which has been protected from freezing.

c. Vehicles should not be repeatedly moved between heated garages and cold outside air; abrupt temperature changes of any kind should be avoided whenever possible. Fuel tanks should be kept filled when possible. The effect of condensation in fuel tanks may be neutralized by the addition of ½-pint ethyl alcohol at each refueling, to absorb the water. Glass enclosed electric defrosters should be used on windshields not equipped with defrosting equipment connected to the vehicle heating system. Cellophane taped to the windshield may be used as a temporary expedient.

d. Optical instruments should not be brought directly into warm quarters when not in use and should be protected from ice and snow while being transported or left exposed.

(1) The lenses and prisms of cold optical equipment fog up when brought indoors. This fogging, which is due to condensation of moisture on lenses, should be removed with lens tissue paper. Any ice which forms on lenses when outdoors, should be removed by use of lens tissue paper wetted with alcohol.

(2) The exposed surfaces of optical elements also fog up when placed close to the face, due to condensation of moisture in the breath. The use of a face mask is the most satisfactory method of keeping the breath away from the oculars. The mask should absorb the moisture from the breath or deflect the breath from the lens. No antifog solution has been found satisfactory for use on lenses at low temperature. Above prevention measures are the only satisfactory remedy.

e. Condensation of breath in microphones and telephone transmitters may be avoided by fastening tissue paper over the openings; otherwise the diaphragm may freeze.

78

96. Freezing to Ground.

Matériel standing in the snow may freeze to the ground. Moving it by force may cause damage to the tires, packing cases or parts of the matériel; loosening it by mechanical means such as chipping, takes time. It is advisable to avoid this freezing by preventive measures such as the use of a coating of nonadherent material or by placing the equipment on a mat of some kind. Metal parts may be coated with grease, which will not stick to ice. Wheels, boxes, track treads, and material affected by grease, can be left standing on tar paper, building paper, straw, a mat of boughs or other similar protection.

97. Fluids and Lubricants.

a. Recoil mechanisms must contain the type of recoil fluid prescribed by the appropriate technical publication. They should be inspected and exercised more frequently as temperatures fail, to prevent sticking, which may result in severe damage. At times the recoil cycle may be slow when firing is begun, due to thickened oil. However, continued firing gradually heats the recoil oil until normal recoil time is obtained.

b. Engine oil used in crankcases will be diluted only as permitted by the pertinent technical manual. Other lubricants will not be diluted, as lubricants prescribed for subzero temperatures provide satisfactory operation when applied in accordance with instructions. Thickened or congealed lubricant on the recoil slides interferes with proper recoil action; therefore, preservative lubrication oil (special) should be used at low temperatures. If this oil is not available, preservative lubricating oil (light) or aircraft and machine gun lubricating oil may be substituted.

98. Coolants.

a. Antifreeze compound (ethylene glycol type) is the only antifreeze authorized for use in automotive cooling systems. The freezing point of water can be lowered by the addition of antifreeze, down to 60° below zero, at a strength of 60 percent antifreeze and 40 percent water. The addition of more antifreeze begins to raise the freezing point, thus reducing its usefulness.

b. Diesel fuel oil or engine oil SAE 10 may be used as coolant in water cooled machine guns. A mixture of glycerin or alcohol with water may also be used. In an emergency only, salt water may be used as a machine gun coolant. It should be removed as soon as possible as it corrodes metal surface during prolonged use.

99. Precautions.

a. Field-strip rifles and remove all rust-preventive compound. Lubricate all parts with preservative lubricating oil (special). When the rifle grenade is fired with the rifle butt resting on the frozen ground, a cloth pad may be used to absorb the shock to the stock.

b. Set gas ports on Browning automatic rifles to widest opening. Wipe machine guns, pistols and submachine guns free of compound and oil lightly with preservative lubricating oil (special). Remove felt oiled pads of the Thompson machine gun.

c. Emplace guns on boughs or mats for firing and pad trail spades to reduce shock from frozen ground and prevent damage to equipment.

d. Cover ammunition in storage and store it off the ground. Remove ice or moisture before firing.

e. Gears must be free before use. Do not force frozen gears. If gears are exposed remove ice with brush. Gears that cannot be cleaned in this manner should be worked gently back and forth to crack or melt the ice.

f. For complete information on cold weather lubrication of artillery, see appropriate technical publications.

100. Expansion and Contraction Effects.

Metals contract or expand as the temperature is lowered or raised; the greater the change in temperature, the greater the contraction or expansion. Lowering the temperature results in contraction. However, all metals do not contract at the same rate. This leads to binding in some mechanisms and looseness in others. Therefore, adjustments should be made at the appropriate temperature at which the equipment is to be used for reasons indicated below.

a. Binding between dissimilar metals is due to the difference in rate of contraction. If a shaft of one metal is mounted in a bearing of a different metal with a greater rate of contraction, the opening in the bearing will shrink faster than the shaft and cause binding. If the bearing had a lower rate of contraction, excessive clearance would result.

b. Expansion and contraction also effect the efficiency of gear trains mounted in a frame or base of dissimilar material. If the gears are adjusted correctly at room temperature, there will be excessive backlash at low temperatures; in the case of a train of gears, the accumulated backlash may prevent the device from operating satisfactorily.

101. Batteries and Generators.

a. Dry batteries usually fail to give adequate current at temperatures below 20° below zero. Small flashlights can sometimes be kept warm enough to use by carrying in an inside pocket.

b. The efficiency of storage batteries decreases

with decreasing temperatures. At 40° below zero even a fully charged storage battery becomes practically inoperative. Batteries must be warmed either by a heater or by remaining in a warm room before they will deliver much power. Batteries should be kept fully charged as a fully charged battery will not freeze at temperatures normally encountered. It is therefore necessary to check batteries frequently and maintain the charge. Do not add water to a battery at subzero temperatures unless it is to be charged immediately or put into use for at least an hour. Otherwise the water will remain on top and freeze.

c. Congealed warm weather oil in the bearings of hand generators and other electrical devices reduces their efficiency. Improved performance will result when bearings are lubricated with prescribed subzero lubricants. Greater ease of operation will be obtained by keeping the equipment in heated tents or vehicles.

102. Drying Clothing.

Shoe leather becomes stiff and cracks if dried in too close proximity to the fire. Wet shoes may be dried by filling them with *warm* oats, corn, or gravel. If the filling is *hot,* stiffness and cracking of the leather will probably result. Maintenance of clothing and shoes in an excellent state of repair is especially important. The necessity for drying clothing after it has become wet cannot be overemphasized. For details on care of clothing see TM 10–275.

103. Snowshoes and Skis.

For care and maintenance of snowshoes and skis, see TM 10–275.

Section II.

WINTERIZATION OF AUTOMOTIVE EQUIPMENT

104. General.

The starting and operation of motor vehicles in extreme cold involves many problems. Certain special equipment is provided to insure proper vehicle protection and satisfactory operation. In addition, proper winter lubricants and lubricating procedures must be used.

105. Winterization Kits.

a. Information concerning winterization kits is available in appropriate technical publication (see FM 21–6).

b. All command and liaison vehicles should be inclosed. Plywood and shipping cases should be saved for this purpose.

106. Lubrication and Lubricants.

For complete information on cold weather lubrication and service of combat vehicles and automotive matériel, see applicable technical publications.

Chapter 11

TACTICAL OPERATIONS

Section I. INFLUENCING FACTORS

107. General.

a. Tactical operations in snow and extreme cold do not vary in principle from those under any other conditions. There are, however, certain differences in their application resulting from these peculiar conditions, which are described in this manual. For a discussion of tactical principles and their general application, see FM 100–5 and the appropriate Field Manuals of the arms and services.

b. References have been made continuously throughout this manual to expedients, methods, and special equipment to be used in areas of snow and extreme cold. In the paragraph 108 their direct application to tactical operations are briefly covered.

108. Influence of Snow and Extreme Cold.

a. Rates of travel for troops and transportation are greatly altered by winter conditions. Deep snow stops cavalry and wheeled vehicles. It also prevents the movement of troops on foot, as well as in armored vehicles, other than those of special design. In open terrain and under favorable snow conditions, infantry on skis has greater mobility than foot troops operating on roads. Oversnow vehicles properly used give units greater cross-country mobility than they would otherwise possess.

b. Snow acts as either an obstacle or an avenue of approach, depending on the equipment and training of the command. Frozen ground makes passageways, instead of obstacles, of swamps, streams, and lakes. Deep snowdrifts and icy slopes restrict movement. Emplacements and field works are difficult to construct, necessitating the use of thawing or explosives.

c. Tracks and installations are more apparent to aerial observers and camouflage is both more difficult and of greater importance than usual. Unless wheeled vehicles are supplanted, or supplemented by oversnow vehicles, supply routes will be canalized to roads and trails. Some canalization will occur in any case, because trails must be used for oversnow equipment, snow shoers, and skiers if speed of movement is to be maintained.

d. For troops who have completed their unit and combined training, considerable training in snow and cold is necessary before a unit is proficient under such conditions; during this training, cross-country movements without shelter in buildings during halts must be practiced. On the march, individuals should be equipped to be self-sustaining, carrying their own food and shelter.

e. While friendly personnel are weakened in strength and morale by cold, fatigue and hunger, this is equally true of the enemy. Whenever possible, the enemy should be denied the use of towns or buildings. Patrols, aircraft and harassing fire should be used against him in bivouacs, and constant raids should prey on his supply system. Every possible means should be employed to deprive him of food, rest, and shelter. He will make corresponding efforts against our troops, and means of repulsing these efforts must be employed.

109. Estimate of Weather and Terrain.

a. The commander is responsible for gathering all data pertinent to the weather, climate, and terrain of the area in which he expects to operate. This information may be obtained from the weather division of the Army Air Forces, weather reports, maps, conversation with friendly natives and with troops who have operated in the area, or other available sources. Specially trained meteorological personnel either organic or attached to the larger units, are extremely valuable.

b. Anticipation of the lowest possible temperatures for the region will be of great importance in the planning of winterization measures, the requisition of proper supplies and equipment, and training of troops. Evaluation of snow depth to be encountered will determine types and amounts of equipment to be employed and will be important in determining the arms and services to be employed, and the proportion of each.

c. Compass declination is greater and more variable in higher latitudes, and is affected by local conditions. Check points should be selected, at which the degree of declination can be verified.

Section II. ORGANIZATION AND EQUIPMENT

110. Special Organization.

Most units of the Army are organized for operation in the weather and terrain usually encountered in temperate zones. Changes of organization are necessary for operations over snow in cold weather. A large part of the troops will operate on snowshoes, but a substantial portion of specially trained ski troops is necessary. Each rifle company will need at least one platoon of ski troops, with larger units of ski troops for the battalion and regiment. Reconnaissance troops of divisions should be replaced by ski troops. The proportion of engineers and service troops will be higher than normal because of the increased need for supplies, and because of the more immediate consequences of supply failures. Troops, native to the region or to a similar region, should be used as scouts and guerillas, since they are able to live, in a large measure, off the country.

111. Storage of Excess Equipment.

Much of the equipment normally used will be burdensome in oversnow operations, particularly away from road nets. Only the bare essentials should be taken into the field. Heavy tentage and stoves for drying and warming should be restricted to the amount and number sufficient to warm about one-third of the troops at a time. In addition to drying, company cooking will be possible only for units in reserve or behind the lines; field ranges in excess of absolute needs should not be taken into the forward areas. Motorized equipment having little oversnow mobility should not be taken into forward areas. Individual and organizational equipment should be carefully checked to eliminate all excess weight. It may be necessary to reduce the number of heavy weapons. It is better to have a few weapons with sufficient ammunition than to have large numbers with insufficient ammunition. Excess organizational and individual equipment should be left with the rear echelon. Training and careful planning will determine the required equipment and avoid wastage of equipment.

112. Supply.

The importance of adequate supply is increased by

cold weather, when maintenance of life is more immediately dependent upon the uninterrupted supply of food and replacement articles of clothing, and shelter. Men can survive for comparatively long periods in' the field in mild weather without adequate food and without clothing replacements; however, at 40° below zero food must be supplied and defective clothing replaced immediately, or casualties will result. The bulk of supplies and the need therefor increases while the means for transporting them decrease. In addition to the usual impediments to supply, enemy action will more often be directed at supply systems than during operations under ordinary conditions. These conditions require the maintenance in forward establishments of the highest level of supply, the dispersion and special protection of supply points, and the existence of alternate and supplementary supply plans. All forms of ground supply should be used; in addition, aerial supply of front-line units may frequently be necessary.

113. Weapons.

a. In selecting weapons for oversnow operations, light weapons, and ammunition should be substituted for heavy weapons and ammunition wherever possible. The organizational heavier weapons can be left with the rear echelon, and brought forward if needed. In heavily wooded terrain, carbines may be substituted for rifles. Mortars and pack howitzers may be substituted for regimental and divisional artillery when operating in rough snow-covered terrain. Automatic antiaircraft weapons may be substituted for the heavier guns, automatic rifles for light machine guns, and light machine guns for heavy machine guns.

b. Ammunition supply will usually be difficult,

but can be aided by reducing the number of weapons used and utilizing all personnel thus released as carrying parties. Inclusion of oversnow vehicles, drawing sleds and troughs for artillery transportation is important. Lack of suitable oversnow transport will force guns to be emplaced near roads; this leads to their early discovery and neutralization. During lulls in work, all available service troops should be sent forward carrying ammunition, to avoid the depletion of front-line units employed for this purpose.

Section III. ARMS AND SERVICES

114. Infantry.

a. Aside from its normal employment, infantry properly trained as ski troops becomes a highly mobile fighting force. Because of frequent use of ski units on patrols and operation behind enemy lines, these units should have better than average military training and should be picked for such missions with particular regard to their physique and condition (ch. 6 and app. II). Ski troops should be especially proficient in map reading, sketching, orientation, observation, demolitions, and scouting and patroling. Maintenance of constant march rates should be stressed.

b. Infantry troops using snowshoes will comprise the bulk of the forces. Properly trained and hardened they should be capable of nearly the same daily marches as foot troops on roads, even though carrying heavier loads. They are not capable, however, of making forced marches of as great duration as foot troops in temperate zones. In addition, their daily rate of march may be reduced by the necessity for personnel to break trail when oversnow equipment is not available for the purpose.

c. Infantry units will operate more patrols than normally. Small units will frequently operate without support. Great stress on individual and small unit training is necessary.

115. Cavalry.
When the snow depth is less than 12 inches, horse cavalry can be used. In extreme cold, precautions must be taken to prevent horses from freezing their lungs. Horse cavalry is not an arm recommended for use in extreme cold and snow because of its limited oversnow ability, the weight and bulk of its forage and the excessive amount of care needed by the animals.

116. Armored Units.
Armored units move cross-country with facility when the ground is thoroughly frozen and there is little snow. Streams and other bodies of water can be crossed when frozen to sufficient thickness to carry the weight of vehicles. Vehicles of the track-laying type can operate in snow which is packed sufficiently to provide traction, but unless they are equipped with extra wide treads and have a high clearance and smooth underbody, their use is restricted to snow of 24 inches or less in depth.

117. Artillery.
a. Oversnow vehicles drawing troughs are a recommended means of transporting artillery in snow-covered terrain. Deep snow prevents the movement of wheeled prime movers or of wheeled carriages. Self-propelled guns are valuable in snow of little

depth. Snow plows will be useful, no matter how the guns are propelled. Sleds or toboggans should be available to carry ammunition and lay wire. Special tools and explosives should be in readiness to prepare emplacements. Camouflage measures should accompany each step of reconnaissance, selection, and occupation of position. Since trails cannot be concealed, they should lead to dummy positions located in a logical position. Tape for marking paths should be put up before the arrival of troops. Mortars may be employed by artillery units as substitute equipment.

b. In addition to firing data for normal targets, data for every ice-covered body of water within range should be calculated. Fire on ice-covered bodies of water, particularly by mortars, is very effective in trapping troops crossing the ice or in suddenly converting a frozen body of water into an obstacle. Long-range harassing fire against enemy supply systems and bivouacs will be normal.

118. Antiaircraft Artillery.
The canalization of supply and communication routes, and the dependence of troops on shelter, make air attack probable and profitable. Roads are continuous defiles for wheeled vehicles. Antiaircraft weapons should accompany trains and convoys and be capable of being fired while moving. In addition supply points and bivouacs need protection. Automatic weapons should be employed whenever possible, as their oversnow mobility is greater than that of antiaircraft guns, and their ammunition is lighter.

119. Engineers.
Engineer troops usually constitute a greater proportion of the total force than is normal for opera-

tions in temperate zones. They should be proficient in bridging open streams at temperatures lower than 40° below zero, clearing roads and railroads of snow, building winter roads and trails, using ice, constructing emplacements, and erecting obstacles in frozen earth and snow-covered terrain. The rate of cross-country movement of the command will be chiefly governed by the proficiency of the attached engineers in overcoming obstacles. In making their plans, engineer officers must know the nature of obstacles, and the temperatures and snow conditions, to be expected. Large track-laying tractors and bulldozers are especially valuable to engineers in cold weather operations. Frozen ground and deep snow reduce the effectiveness of small or medium tractors and bulldozers.

120. Signal Corps.

Most signal equipment can be used in low temperatures if the difficulties peculiar to cold are anticipated and the means of overcoming them are known.

a. Wire laying is difficult in cold weather, and tractor-drawn, wire-laying cargo sleds are desirable. Hand reels should be mounted on small sleds or toboggans. For messenger and wire inspection service, men should be trained in the use of skis. Recovery of wire in snow by combat troops is usually impracticable. An extra supply must be carried for this reason. At unheated message centers, extra items of warm clothing should be on hand to throw over runners and messengers while they are awaiting further duties.

b. For operational use, electrical signal equipment should be located in warm rooms or shelters. At halts, it may be necessary to build fires to warm electrical equipment. Batteries can be kept warm under clothing or blankets. An extra supply of batteries is essential.

c. Frozen soil does not make a good ground. Grounds should be placed below the frost line in cellars and wells where possible.

d. Colored signal panels, preferably orange, are highly visible.

e. Because of the difficulties of messenger communication, full use must be made of other available means of communication.

f. Pigeons have been used successfully in extreme cold; however, large owls, hawks and eagles, all natural enemies of pigeons, abound in most cold weather areas. Pigeons also are hindered by the ground fogs prevalent in still air when the temperature is lower than 35° below zero.

121. Chemical Warfare.

Smoke hangs low in cold weather and is very effective. Colored smokes are particularly conspicuous against snow backgrounds. The supply of chemicals should be limited to those which will volatilize at the temperatures encountered. An increase in consumption of incendiaries, screening smokes, signal smokes and fire starters is to be anticipated. Chemical emergency fire starters should be procured and issued freely to field units.

122. Quartermaster Corps.

a. Cold and snow make the shelter of some items of the ration imperative. Freezing alone does not unduly harm perishable items of the ration, but alternate freezing and thawing will quickly spoil them. Underground storage bins may be necessary. Increase of rations must be allowed for in planning operations in snow and cold. Rations may be lost or damaged in air dropping. Torn or damaged clothing and equipment must be replaced without delay. Laundry and bathing facilities are more important than in warmer areas, as fewer substitutes for them exist, and cleanliness is necessary to preserve warmth and reduce vermin infestation. Bakeries are more difficult to operate but, once they are operating, bread may be frozen as fast as baked, and stored in cold with excellent results. The bread will remain fresh indefinitely if frozen.

b. Procurement of local varieties of draft animals and their handlers and equipment may become necessary.

123. Ordnance.

a. Provision must be made for the supply, maintenance, and repair of oversnow vehicles which may be substituted for wheeled vehicles. Movable parts of weapons equipment exposed to cold and strains may require higher replacement factors than normal. The procurement of adequate cold weather lubricants and recoil fluids must be planned.

b. Any necessary modification of weapons and equipment should be made before the beginning of operations.

124. Army Air Forces.

a. Combat aviation targets remain unchanged under conditions of extreme cold or deep snow. Snowstorms and low-hanging fog restrict the use of airplanes. Below 35° below zero, low ground fogs are quite prevalent.

b. Increased calls for supply dropping missions are also to be anticipated. Normally, supplies are dropped by parachute on such missions. Free dropping of supplies (dropping without parachutes) is practical in deep snow when the dropping area is indicated and friendly troops are present.

Section IV. LEADERSHIP AND COMMAND

125. Effect of Cold on Morale.

Cold produces lethargy, apathy, and slow and clumsy reactions which are accentuated by bulky clothing. Depression and discouragement, and a firm conviction that they are doing more than their share of the necessarily heavy work, are present in the minds of many individuals. These feelings are intensified in the cold weather of higher latitudes where the hours of darkness are longer. Leaders must combat these mental conditions by provision of warming and drying facilities, and insure that their use is rotated evenly among all troops. Hot foods should be provided at least twice a day, preferably morning and evening. Work for the succeeding day should be planned ahead and work assignments made the night before. Care must be taken to make certain that work is rotated.

126. Advance Planning.

a. Advance planning is of great importance in cold weather operations. Leaders should attempt to learn everything possible about the area of operations, including such items as the type of clothing, shelter, and transportation used by the natives of the region.

b. Accurate estimates of the weather to be encountered and the effects of weather on the terrain must be made and disseminated to staff officers. The type of cold, whether wet or dry, must be determined, as clothing and winterization measures differ radically. Wet cold has not been emphasized in this manual, as it is rarely extreme cold, although its effect on men may be severe. In wet cold, waterproof clothing must be worn and heavy greases and lubricants used in quantity. Areas in which wet cold is to be encountered are the Aleutians, the Kurile Islands, and some parts of the Baltic and North Sea areas.

c. A cadre of personnel having experience in cold weather is desirable for training troops in cold weather procedure. Visits by the commander and his staff to places where terrain and climate are similar to those of the contemplated area of operations are helpful. Officers and men alike must cultivate a thorough respect for the casualty-producing power of cold, but should not fear it.

127. Supervision

The supervision which is always necessary assumes even greater importance in operations in snow and extreme cold. Wearing apparel must be prescribed and its method of wear supervised. Camps or bivouacs must be planned in detail, and their construction supervised to insure equality of work and comfort for all. Troops must be supervised on the march, and told when to remove clothing and replace it to avoid sweating and chilling. Food and shelter must be inspected for adequacy. As the state of cold weather discipline and training increases, much of this supervision may be delegated to subordinates.

128. Administration.

Faulty administration is a greater handicap to the operational abilities of troops in cold weather than in temperate weather. Delays are far more serious in cold weather, and must be avoided.

Section V. RECONNAISSANCE AND INTELLIGENCE

129. General.

a. Snow-covered terrain makes the concealment of activity within an area virtually impossible. Because the enemy will find it difficult to conceal evidence of his presence, he may be expected to make every effort to mislead our forces as to his strength, composition, and exact location. This increases the necessity for effective reconnaissance and the importance of combat intelligence. Reconnaissance is hindered by the ground fogs encountered at temperatures around 40° below zero or lower, snow storms, drifting snow, heavy woods, and the longer hours of darkness and poor light characteristic of winter in higher latitudes. It is aided by the better transmission of sound in cold air, the manner in which smoke hangs without dispersion in cold clear air, the difficulty of concealing activity in snow-covered terrain, and the value of the long shadows cast in winter time. It must be borne in mind that conditions affecting the operations of friendly intelligence apply with equal force to those of the enemy.

b. For detailed discussion of reconnaissance and intelligence, see FM 100–5, and Field Manuals in the 30– series.

130. Combat Intelligence.

a. AIR RECONNAISSANCE. The success of air reconnaissance depends on clear weather. Ground haze completely obscures enemy activity from the camera, and nearly so from the eyes of the observer. A heavy fall of snow covers all surface marks. In clear weather, however, the detailed information to be gained from the air makes it possible to deduce from tracks and installations a great deal about the enemy's equipment, strength, and location. Interpretation of aerial photographs is very important in snow operations. Photographs should be taken frequently during periods of enemy activity to show emplacements before muzzle blast marks can be covered, and before signs of other activity in suspected areas can be concealed. They should also be taken under varying conditions of light, snowfall, and thawing, as camouflage is easier to detect when large numbers of photographs of the area under different conditions are available. Route reconnaissance may be accomplished by use of liaison aircraft.

b. GROUND RECONNAISSANCE. Air reconnaissance should be supplemented by ground reconnaissance. Air reconnaissance can usually furnish negative information concerning enemy presence in a given area by reason of lack of tracks, but if the snow surface is broken, ground reconnaissance is needed to ascertain definitely the presence or absence, strength, composition, location and dispositions of the enemy. This is also true in localities where aerial observation of the snow surface is prevented by vegetation. Track-laying oversnow vehicles are useful for reconnaissance in rough or lightly wooded terrain and deep powdery snow; they are useless in thick woods. Ski troops are very useful for reconnaissance if they are well trained in cross-country work. They have high mobility, are easily hidden, and are silent. The assignment of specially trained ski troops to units for reconnaissance should be made.

c. DECEPTIVE ENEMY TACTICS. The difficulties of concealment may induce the enemy to attempt deception by preparing false positions and by making misleading tracks over large areas. Whenever possible, the tracks made by reconnaissance parties should be obscured, in order that the strength of the parties may be concealed. Old tracks may be used, but care should be taken to insure that they are not mined. It may be advisable for a reconnaissance party to mine its own tracks. Whether or not this is done, the likelihood of enemy discovery makes it inadvisable to return by the same route.

d. ADDITIONAL DUTIES OF GROUND RECONNAISSANCE. In addition to securing normal tactical information, reconnaissance will be required to establish:

(1) The condition of the snow away from the roads.

(2) The condition and width of roads and tracks.

(3) The thickness of ice over water obstacles that our own vehicles may be required to cross, and the suitability of these obstacles for delaying the enemy.

(4) The presence of other obstacles and of concealed traps.

(5) The danger of avalanches.

(6) Bivouac sites.

e. TRANSMISSION OF INFORMATION. The information obtained by reconnaissance detachments can be passed back rapidly by establishing a message center to which pairs of skiers bring reports from the forward detachments. Information is sent back from the message center by whatever means of communication are available.

f. ROAD MARKING. Reconnaissance parties may be required to mark tracks or roads. In mountains, they can be marked by blazing trees or with rocks, while in open snow country poles, flags, or snow markers can be used. Stakes are used to mark the ends of roads.

g. CONSERVING ENERGY OF PATROLS. Movement through snow is exhausting, and reconnaissance patrols may have to travel long distances. Ski troops should be saved fatigue whenever possible by taking them to their starting point by skijoring (towing by horses or snow tractors) or in vehicles. Troops should not normally be employed on active reconnaissance duties for more than 24 hours continuously.

131. Interpretation.

Tracks in the snow reveal the strength of the enemy and the type of equipment used. His location may be deduced from the smoke haze which hangs low over fires in extremely cold weather, and by the indications of recent use of trails. In still air, conversations and the noise of woodcutting will carry long distances. In winter, shadows are longer and make aerial photo interpretation easier. In estimating enemy capabilities it is important to realize that the means at his disposal are not necessarily the same as those at the disposal of our forces.

132. Countermeasures.

Since tracks cannot be concealed, they should be

made to mislead the enemy by leading to camouflaged dummy positions, logically situated. Silence must be observed and no fires lighted if an attempt to conceal the presence of our troops is to be made. Wood should be sawed rather than chopped when near the enemy. Every position should be provided all-around security to include ski patrols when appropriate. Likely avenues of approach for over-snow equipment and skis should be kept under surveillance. Camouflage must be assiduously practiced.

Section VI. SECURITY
133. On the March.
Some ski troops must be assigned to advance, flank, and rear guards. The bulk of the ski troops, because of their mobility, should be held as a reserve. The flanks and rear of moving columns are targets for attacks by enemy ski troops. Engineers in considerable strength, should be allotted to the advance guard. Liaison aircraft may be employed if available to observe for signs of enemy activity to the front, flanks, and rear. Advance and flank guards should be relieved frequently, since their missions are fatiguing. Advance guards should be relieved by leap-frogging at halts; flank guards should be assigned phase lines between which they must cover the main body, and then rejoin.

134. Halts and Bivouacs.
a. Units in bivouacs in snow or extreme cold should be dispersed as in any operations. Bivouacs are prime targets for small enemy ski detachments. Ski detachments approaching to just within mortar range of a bivouac and firing mortar shells into it are especially troublesome; every effort should be made to prevent such close approach.

b. Ski patrols should visit outguards by circular routes, identifying themselves by the proper challenge, password, and reply at each sentry post on each visit. Patrols should check for trails breaking across the circumference of their route; entry and exit should be at one point only. Sentry posts should consist of three men, with a sentinel continuously posted. Sentries should be relieved at frequent intervals. The two men not on post can be in their sleeping bags. In bivouacs, it may be necessary to sleep in the sleeping bags fully clothed, as it would be fatal to be driven from sleeping bags partially dressed in extremely low temperature. The practice of sleeping clothed is ordinarily inadvisable, but is necessary in proximity to the enemy.

c. Patrols should operate not only on the outguard circumference, but also between the outguards and the bivouac area. Offensive patrols should also be sent out toward the enemy, leaving and returning from definite places. Surrounding areas should be carefully checked from the air just before dark to discover any enemy movement toward friendly areas.

135. Antimechanized Security.

a. In extreme cold, streams, swampy ground, and lakes may cease to be antitank barriers. Swampy ground becomes firm, and water barriers may be crossed at some or all points, depending on the stream. Deep, powdery snow forms the best barrier. Snow on slopes forms a greater obstacle than do the slopes themselves. Slopes can be iced to form good antimechanized barriers. Special type tanks having extra wide treads, of light weight, and with good clearance can, however, traverse deep snow. Woods and snow combined provide excellent antimechanized security. Snow covering makes antitank mines harder to detonate. Gasoline incendiary grenades are very inefficient, as are frangible gas grenades, because the low temperature prevents rapid vaporization of the contents on which the action of these grenades depends.

b. Antitank guns usually will be fewer in number and of lighter types under conditions of deep snow because of difficulty of transportation. They can be transported by towing in troughs, or hauled on toboggans. Light antitank guns can be mounted in track-laying oversnow vehicles and serve both for their primary mission against tanks, and also for missions against miscellaneous point targets (see FM 7-35).

136. Antiaircraft Security.

Antiaircraft security measures must be intensified because of the greater likelihood of air attacks and the relatively greater effect of these attacks in cold weather. The canalization of lines of communication, the necessity for uninterrupted supply, and the difficulty in camouflaging supply points favor enemy air attack. The remedies for these conditions are the substitution of oversnow vehicles for wheeled vehicles and the movement of oversnow vehicles by individual routes, dispersion of supply points, with a relatively higher level of supply in forward installations than normal, camouflage of supply points and use of false trails, and the protection of columns and supply points by antiaircraft fire. Air superiority in a given area is not a guarantee of safety, as the profit to ,the enemy of air attack on lines of communication may outweigh his probable loss in planes.

137. Antichemical Security.

The danger of attack by chemicals is limited by the temperatures at which various chemicals vaporize; the importance of chemical security drops with the temperature, except when occupying areas formerly held by the enemy. When chemicals have been used in an area, the snow surface is usually discolored. Low temperatures make all chemicals more persistent than normal, but less effective. Some chemical indicators do not function in extreme low temperatures, but this disadvantage is offset by the relative ineffectiveness of chemical agents at such temperatures.

Section VII. MOVEMENTS

138. General.

a. MARCHING. Marching personnel are exposed to freezing, are slowed by snow, are fatigued greatly by trail breaking and carrying a heavier-than-normal pack, and are subject to becoming lost in snow storms. The great physical exertion required causes dehydration and acute thirst.

b. AIR. Air movements require the least exertion, and are independent of snow conditions except at points of take off and landing. If gliders are used, troops can easily be transported to points having no available plane landing fields.

c. RAIL. Rail movements necessitate the use of snow plows for track clearance, the heating of cars, and the incorporation of antiaircraft units in the train. Rolling stock should be inspected for comfort before commencing the movement, and a heat source provided for each car if passenger cars are not used.

d. MOTOR. Motor movements of troops in snow and extreme cold require road clearance, winterization of vehicles, cover and insulation for truck bodies, use of lugs and chains, provisions for tactical security for the convoy, and frequent halts.

e. OVERSNOW. Oversnow vehicles are not well suited to hauling large numbers of men. They are usually best suited for short range movement. Personnel should be dressed very warmly when riding in these vehicles.

f. RATES. Rates of movement, except for troops mounted on skis, are much slower in snow than in areas clear of snow. This applies to marching, rail movements, and the movement of wheeled transport. In unbroken snow, trails must be broken or roads opened. Passing zones, parking areas on shoulders for stalled vehicles, and turn-arounds, must be cleared when roads are opened.

g. HALTS. (1) Halts must be frequent and of short duration when men are exposed to the cold. Hot drinks should be served whenever possible. No halt should be made for the *preparation* of the noon meal, as this wastes the brief daylight; noon meals of prepared rations may be eaten by personnel while moving. Routes should be planned to afford the greatest possible speed between points, and bivouac areas should be reached before men are exhausted. Routes should also be planned to necessitate as litle trail breaking as possible, and to avoid defiles and steep slopes. For train and truck movements the entire route is a continuous defile. Snowshoes and skis should be carried with individual equipment on such movements, otherwise deployment in snow is impossible.

(2) Periods of relatively high temperatures, accompanied by snowfall or melting, may occur between periods of extreme cold. If clothing and equipment become wet during a warm period, it is imperative that the command be halted immedi-

ately and clothing and equipment dried completely, before continuing the march. In addition, halts
for drying of sleeping bags and clothing will be
necessary about once in five to ten days, as these
articles absorb moisture from the body more rapidly than they exude it.

139. Road Marking.

a. In winter, snowfalls, fog, and snowdrifts frequently make roads and terrain features unrecog-
nizable. Therefore, careful road marking is essential. If possible, through roads must be uniformly
marked prior to the first snowfall. Road designa-
tions must be known to troops who will use the
routes. Permanent routes should be designated by
durable markers.

b. In open country, poles about 8 feet high with
direction markers, snow markers, wisps of straw,
brushwood, rock cairns, and flags serve the purpose.

c. Orientation is facilitated if the markers are
numbered in the direction of march, and if they
are placed at equal distances from each other. Road
markers must be erected at least three feet off the
trail in order to avoid damage by traffic. In wooded
terrain, tree trunks are marked with blazes, plac-
ards, or paint; branches are bent; boards, paper,
or cloth remnants are fastened to trees.

d. If complete road marking is impossible, arrow
signposts should be erected at prominent points to
indicate the direction of march and distance to the
objective. For short distances, direction arrows will
be sufficient.

e. Road markers which have been in use for
long periods must be checked because their position
may be changed by the enemy. If routes are
changed, the distances indicated on the markers
must be revised.

f. Simple marks in the snow, snow markers, and similar signs are adequate for the marking of temporary roads, such as those used by patrols. If strange trails cross the route, they must be obliterated within the immediate vicinity of friendly tracks so that the troops will not go astray. It is frequently advisable to leave guards at such points in order to keep units on the proper route.

140. Road Making.

a. GENERAL. (1) If an engineer unit with special type equipment, such as bulldozers or snow tractors, is attached to a unit, the task of building winter roads devolves upon the engineers, assisted, if necessary, by other troops; otherwise, road making must be done by any available troops.

(2) In snowy terrain it is frequently easier to construct and maintain new roads at favorable locations (for instance, to by-pass defiles) than to clear existing roads. It will frequently be necessary to cut new cross-country roads (for evading the enemy, bringing heavy weapons into position and other purposes). Roads in snow-covered, pathless terrain may be cut by small trail details which speed ahead on skis to mark the route and by larger road construction detachments on foot. In winter warfare all units should organize, equip, and train trail details and road construction detachments.

b. ROUTES FOR TACTICAL PURPOSES. In establishing routes for tactical purposes, the following types of terrain and approaches are most suitable: flat country, plateaus, sparsely wooded land, forest paths protected from the wind, frozen rivers, lakes, swamps, and existing field paths. Across open country, trails should be laid preferably along telegraph lines, fences, and similar installations. Terrain which is exposed to snowdrifts is less suitable; for this reason, routes should be established from 300 to 500 feet from the edges of woods. Heavily wooded terrain is difficult, and should be by-passed whenever possible. This is also true of insufficiently frozen swamps, patches of melting ice, snow-filled hollows, deep ravines, gorges, defiles, and steep slopes. Obstacles around which snowdrifts may form (for instance, farm buildings, piles of stones, and brushwood) must be removed or by-passed at a distance equal to 10 times their height. On inclines steeper than 10 percent, trails must be cut in serpentine fashion, oblique to the slope. Curves must be made as wide as possible; sharp curves are more difficult for sleds than for wheeled vehicles.

c. DEVELOPMENT OF ROAD. When trails are being reconnoitered and plotted, it must be decided whether the roadway eventually is to be a one-lane or a two-lane artery. At first only a one-lane section is constructed. Bypasses wide enough for two sleds are later added; they should be at least 50 feet long. Finally, the road may be enlarged to make a two-lane artery. A double lane is preferable to two separate lanes because the latter are less efficient in case of traffic jams and snow drifts.

d. METHODS. (1) The method of making roads depends upon the type of traffic the roads will have to bear, upon the depth of the snow, and the equipment available. Ski trails cut by a trail detail will suffice for small ski detachments which use only man-hauled sleds. Larger units with motor-drawn sleds will require a road-construction detachment. Trail details should start about one hour ahead of a marching column. Road-construction detachments need a start of several hours, depending upon the length of the road to be cut. The following table illustrates the method of operation of a road construction detachment of one officer and 34 men:

TRAIL-BREAKING DETACHMENT TABLE

Designation	Strength	Mission	Equipment
Trail-blazing detail on skis.	1 officer, 6 to 12 EM.	Under command of an experienced officer, the detail plots the trail, straightens curves and grades rough spots, removes small obstacles such as branches, and marks the route.	Compass, wire-cutters, ice auger, crowbar, ice measuring stick, 2 axes, marking equipment, skis, 50 feet ¾-inch rope.
Trail-blazing group without skis.	2 NCO's; 18 EM.	Packs down snow on trail, removes obstacles and cuts away obstructing brushwood and trees, strengthens weak sections of trail, relieves trail-blazing detail.	1 or 2 automatic rifles, and portable in-trenching tools. Other equipment is loaded on sleds.
Lightly loaded sled.	2 EM, 2 horses, or snow tractor.	Cuts the first sled track.	4 shovels, 2 axes, 4 pick-axes, 1 crowbar 1 saw, demolition material, 1 icedrill, instruments for measuring ice capacity.
Heavily loaded sled.	2 or 3 EM, 2 horses, or snow tractor.	Deepens and solidifies the sled track.	6 shovels, 8 axes, 6 pick-axes, 3 crowbars; 3 saws, 1 pair of wire-cutters, 4 ice axes, 1 hammer, 1 pair of pliers, demolition material, construction material, wire.
Sled with tree trunks.	1 NCO, 1 EM, 2 horses, or snow tractor.	Clears snow from foot and vehicular trails.	1 axe, 1 pickax, 1 snow shovel, 5 tree hooks or chains.
Sled with evergreen tree.	2 EM, 2 horses, or snow tractor.	Clears snow from foot and vehicular trails.	1 axe, 1 pickax, 1 snow shovel, 5 tree hooks or chains.

Since newly cut roads are soon damaged at many points by large bodies of marching men, it is advisable to assign a road construction detachment to the head of each column for the purpose of making repairs.

(2) *Breaking trails.* In breaking trails by manpower, the leading man in a file should break trail for a short predetermined distance or time, then step to one side of the trail until the tail of the column of men breaking trail passes him; he should then fall in at the tail of the column. The next man in line automatically begins to break trail. Rotation should occur at very short intervals. Individuals should never be allowed to break trail continuously, as their pace will slacken as they tire, with a resultant delay in the march of the main body.

e. SNOW PLOWS. Snow about 20 inches deep can be cleared with snow plows. For this purpose, the following types may be used in sequence; breaking plows, advance plows, widening plows, and side plows. The breaking plow or advance plow is pushed by horses or drawn by snow tractor. A strong detachment of men must always be allotted to each plow section. They must be equipped with shovels, axes, and pickaxes for the removal of obstacles.

f. HARDENING OF ROAD SURFACES. Roads with 20 inches or more of snow which will be used by heavy traffic can be packed solid with snowrollers. Rollers are preferable to snow plows because they do not create snow banks at the roadside. Another method of hardening road surfaces is to freeze them. Sleds with wooden water tanks are used for this purpose. The tanks must have several openings on the bottom, at the rear, for spraying the water. To prevent the freezing of the water while it is being transported, the tanks must be heated with hot stones or by other means.

141. Winter Road Service.

a. PREPARATIONS. With the beginning of cold weather, winter maintenance must be started on all important roads and paths. Such service is the duty of all troops. Civil inhabitants with horse teams, prisoners of war, and local road services, if any, should be used as much as possible. Regulating and supervising traffic is an essential part of the winter road service, which should be linked with the existing communication net. When the block system of traffic control is used, communications must be installed and maintained between block points. In order to prevent accidents and traffic jams, every individual using the road, especially the drivers of motor vehicles, must adhere to strict road discipline, observe all traffic signs, and obey all orders which may be issued. Posts for road guards must be established along the road, and communication between these posts and headquarters provided. The road guards reconnoiter certain sections of the road before the first snowfall and, after the beginning of freezing weather and snow, again travel over these sections and check their condition. They report immediately the depth of snowfalls and snowdrifts and the location of icy surfaces. Shortly before the first frost sets in, the surface of soft roads is made even by the use of graders, agricultural equipment, and heavy harrows. Later snow-clearing work is considerably facilitated by these measures. Markers are placed at the edge of the road, on both sides if possible. They are attached to milestones, to trees, and to fence rails at points where material for road construction is stocked, and are also put up at passages and obstacles of all kinds. Bypasses are especially marked. Snow fences and antiskid material are stored alongside the road.

b. CLEARING ROADS. Troops will use all available mechanical equipment for clearing roads. Unless sufficient equipment is on hand, a mass employment of manpower is always required after a heavy snowfall. Clearing must be started immediately after the first fall and must be repeated continually. Delay makes the work more difficult. If possible, the road must be cleared down close to its surface. If some snow is to be left for sled traffic, a depth of 1 to 4 inches is sufficient. It is desirable, for the protection of road surfaces, to retain a firm snow cover until the end of freezing weather. Snow cleared from roads must be widely scattered away from road ditches. It must not be piled up, as piling causes new snowdrifts. Deep-rutted snow which has been hardened by traffic or freezing and has an uneven surface can be leveled with agricultural implements. Loose snow is packed into the ruts. Melting snow must be drained far off to the side. Mud must be removed. All traffic signs, especially warnings at railroad crossings, must be shoveled clear and checked continuously.

c. SNOW FENCES. (1) Fences must be used where the natural contours of the terrain cause snowdrifts. The height of fences varies from 4 to 6 feet. They should be erected at a distance from the edge of the road which is 10 to 15 times the height of the fence. They must be vertical and, if possible, at right angles to the direction of the prevailing wind. Information on wind conditions and drift spots should be secured from natives.

(2) Snow fences of two types have proved effective in preventing snowdrifts on roads. When an "accumulation" fence is used, snow piles up on either side of it. "Guide" fences cause the snow to

be swept by the wind at an oblique angle to the road and deposited at a distance from the thoroughfare where it will not interfere with traffic.

(3) If wood for fences is lacking, snow walls made of snow blocks may be substituted. These require constant repair.

d. TREATMENT OF SLIPPERY SURFACES. Slippery snow and ice surfaces should be sprinkled with sand, gravel, or crushed rock. For slippery snow surfaces, a coarser type of antiskid material can be used than for ice, because it is pressed into the snow. The antiskid material must be piled in advance along the roadside. It should contain no earth. The piles must be marked so that they may be found after they are covered with snow. The material is spread immediately after the surface becomes slippery. When the ice crust is chopped or removed, the surface of the road must not be damaged. Two layers of chicken wire, with brush between, and secured with large nails, make an effective device for crossing icy roads.

e. TRANSITION FROM SNOW TO MUD. (1) When, during the transition period from winter to spring, temperatures are above freezing in daytime and below at night, roads are dry and hard only at night and in the morning. Vehicular traffic must, therefore, be limited to these hours. Men whose duty it is to dispatch vehicles must see to it that advantage is taken of the most favorable hours. All drivers, and especially drivers of motor vehicles, must strictly observe traffic discipline. Driving on dirt roads must be avoided to the greatest possible extent unless such roads are completely dry. Traffic during the mud period must be directed to tracks on the left and right of the road.

(2) Water must be drained off the roads. Roads must, therefore, be cleared of snow before the

thaw period so that ditches and culverts can function properly. The drying of dirt roads can be expedited by grading the surfaces. The mud thus removed must not interfere with drainage. Ditches and culverts must be kept open.

(3) In inhabited localities, roads can be graveled by the demolition of stone buildings and breaking up of the stones. Large stones make the road worse; only an even layer of small stones will serve the purpose. Sticks and planks for the construction of corduroy roads, prepared during the frost period, should be on hand along all indispensable supply roads. This applies especially to those sections of road which lead through depressions or valleys, which dry later than roads on high grounds. Sources of sand should be located. Sand should be piled in readiness wherever it may be needed for spreading on wet sections of roads. Lumber for the construction of small bridges should be available at the lowest points on roads and paths.

142. Ice Crossings.

a. CAPACITY OF ICE. The thickness of ice crusts may vary in every body of water. Over river currents, near the banks, and under snow, the ice crust is generally thin. This also applies to swampy ground and warm springs. An ice crust under which the water level has fallen breaks more easily than one resting on the surface of the water. During the thaw period, ice becomes dull and brittle and loses its carrying capacity, and heavy traffic wears it through very quickly. In determining the carrying capacity of ice crusts, not only the thickness, but also the nature of the ice is a factor. Only light, clear ice is a reliable carrier. The familiar dull upper and lower layers must not be considered in estimating its strength. Before venturing on large-

114

scale ice crossings, ample blocks must be cut out and checked for firmness. The load capacity of ice is shown in appendix I. These factors are dependable only when the proper march intervals are observed, and they give only a general idea of the weight which can be sustained by ice surfaces.

b. PREPARATIONS AND SAFETY MEASURES. A crossing must be made on an ice crust of uniform thickness and, if possible, one without holes. Approach and departure roads and some by-passes must also be available. For measuring the thickness of the ice along the crossing, holes are cut at distances of about 10 to 16 feet from the center of the route, and spaced from 33 to 65 feet apart. The crossing and a strip about 20 feet wide on both sides of it are cleared of snow so that the condition of the ice may be watched during the march. Crossings for motor vehicles and foot troops are sprinkled with sand. For sleds, a thin layer of snow should be spread on the ice. The various crossings, roads of approach and departure, and holes, may be marked by small snow walls, railings or poles. The carrying capacity of the ice and the distances to be maintained between vehicles should be clearly shown on posters.

143. Wheeled Vehicle Transport.

a. Truck bodies should be insulated by packing them with sawdust, straw boughs, or other available material. Tarpaulins are either left up with the back curtain in place or are removed entirely and personnel covered individually with shelter halves. The latter measure is necessary in the presence of the enemy in order that men may not be trapped inside trucks. Use of tarpaulins without back flaps causes snow to cover men riding in the truck. Safety from ambush and air attack dictates the use of individual covering rather than the tarpaulin. Snowshoes should be with each individual. Antiaircraft weapons should accompany the column and be capable of firing while moving.

  b. Turn-arounds, passing lanes, and parking areas on roadsides for disabled vehicles are necessary. All trucks should be winterized and should use chains. Lugs should be available for use by the leading vehicles in the convoy. Truck convoys should not enter unreconnoitered defiles.

  c. Motor vehicles with two-wheel drive operate with difficulty on roads in 1 foot of snow. Vehicles with four-wheel drive can usually run on the level in snow up to about 1½ feet deep. Vehicles with caterpillar treads can move through much deeper snow. Snow plows should be available to all troops using roads in winter. Engineer troops will ordinarily be charged with the duty of keeping the roads passable.

  d. Drivers and passengers should avoid direct contact with metal. Metal seats should be well padded. A piece of sheepskin or woolen cloth should be sewed around the steering wheel. The metal handles of tools should be covered with cloth or adhesive tape.

  e. Where streams and lakes are to be crossed, open cabs are safer than closed cabs. The doors of closed cabs should be kept open while crossing ice to prevent the drivers from being trapped in case of a break-through. Troops being transported should dismount and walk across ice. When halted, it is better, when possible, to chock the wheels rather than to set the brakes, since cold and condensed moisture often cause a set brake to lock. When stopping on snow, ice, or frozen ground, brakes should be applied gently. A sudden application of the brakes is likely to cause slipping, loss of control, and accidents. In driving through drifts, the vehicle should be put in low gear and four-wheel drive before entering the drift, and then kept moving. Stopping or slowing up in a drift to change gears often results in stalling.

f. At 30° below zero, Diesel oil becomes too sluggish to flow through pipes. An improvised wood stove made of sheet metal and built against the fuel tank is sometimes useful in warming the oil when starting. After starting, the fuel in most Diesel tractors is kept warm by the engine exhaust.

g. Tractors with wide tracks are reliable and efficient means of transportation. They are not confined to roads, can run over deep snow, knock down small trees, cross rough terrain, pull heavy weapons, sleds or trailers, and climb steep slopes. They travel at a rate of about 6 miles per hour. Preceded by bulldozers, they can make their own roads and are particularly useful where highways are scarce. Each tractor should be equipped with a power-operated winch and heavy duty cable 250 to 300 feet long to move tows over otherwise impassable ground and to lower them down steep slopes. When sleds or other trailers are being towed by tractors, it is usually easier to run over snowdrifts than to clear roads through them. In going down steep slopes with sleds in tandem, brakes may be improvised by wrapping ropes or chains around the runners. Sleds may also be kept from overrunning the tractor by attaching ropes in rear and having men hold them back.

h. Extreme cold slows up the march of motorized or mechanized vehicles because of halts necessary to allow personnel in open or unheated vehicles to dismount and get warm by moving about and restoring circulation. Cold will increase maintenance difficulties which will further slow down the march. Drivers, operators, gunners, and, in fact, all personnel must become accustomed to driving and working on their vehicles in awkward clothing and mittens or gloves.

i. Snow is the chief deterrent to the march of wheeled vehicles. Long marches are extremely fatiguing to drivers unless the trail is well broken. Normal distances can be maintained in snow marching, except in blinding snow, when distances must be reduced. Since there is little likelihood of air observation during a snowfall, the columns may be shortened. The almost constant use of chains or traction devices greatly increases the wear on vehicles and the necessity for adjustments. All personnel must therefore be trained to help the driver inspect the vehicle at every opportunity during the march. They must be alert to detect trouble in the traction devices. Each man should know how to use or improvise emergency expedients to extricate stalled or stuck vehicles. Certain personnel must be familiar with the operation of the snow plows and their upkeep. Heavy vehicles will break trail better than light vehicles. Scout cars can break trail at 15 to 20 miles per hour up to a snow depth of 14 inches. Mechanical strain as well as driver fatigue requires that the leading vehicles be changed frequently. There should be at least two drivers with each vehicle; these alternate in driving.

144. Oversnow Equipment.

The use of oversnow equipment enables the commander to avoid roads and trails and to advance on a wide front. Maximum use of the cross-country mobility of oversnow vehicles should be made at all times to effect deployment. Aerial route reconnaissance will aid in the selection of wide avenues of approach. Track-laying vehicles should tow loads, rather than carry them; the loads on all oversnow vehicles should be kept light. Ski troops can easily be towed behind track-laying vehicles (see app. II). Cooling vents of oversnow vehicles should be left open. Routes should be selected which do not demand the maximum performance of which a vehicle is capable.

145. Rail Transport.

a. Rolling stock should be insulated and heated, and shelters built for the gunners on the antiaircraft flatcars. Tanks, trucks, and animals should be loaded or unloaded only after loading platforms and ramps have been sprinkled with sand. Storage batteries should be removed from vehicles and transported in heated cars, and radiators checked for winterization. Windows and doors of trains should not be allowed to stand open. If stoves are used in train cars, one man should be detailed to watch the stoves at all times to prevent fires or carbon monoxide poisoning.

b. Railroad tracks are especially vulnerable to forays made by ski troops, and should be guarded. A pilot flatcar pushed ahead of the train is additional insurance against placed mines and demolitions. Clearance of tracks and reconnaissance for possible avalanche areas must be accomplished.

c. Railroad transportation is often interrupted by deep snow, drifts, and snowslides. Snowslides occur most frequently in mountainous regions when heavy fresh snow falls over a glazed crust, or during thaws. In deep passes and defiles, snow will often form in drifts 50 or more feet in depth. During melting weather, slides are often started by the vibration from passing trains. They are more apt to occur in the daytime than at night, since the drop in temperature after nightfall often causes a temporary freeze. When thaws are likely to cause snowslides, the safest period for running trains through mountainous districts is between the late hours of the night and sunrise. An ample supply of rotary railroad snow plows should be held in readiness, so located as to permit them to work simultaneously on both ends of probable drifts and slides. The cowcatchers of all locomotives should be provided with plates for clearing light snow from the track. The track should be kept under constant observation so that a timely warning of obstructions may be reported.

Section VIII. OFFENSIVE OPERATIONS

146. General.

a. Oversnow mobility is the ability of a command to move cross country over snow-covered terrain independently of roads and trails. It is attained only by the employment of vehicles—snow tractors, heavy track-laying tractors, tractor trains, sleds—of the proper type and number; and of troops specially trained and equipped to operate in snow and extreme cold.

b. Unless a unit exploits its oversnow mobility to the fullest extent, it will be tied to roads and trails. When a command operates in this fashion, cross-country movements to envelop the enemy become impossible; costly frontal attacks are the alternative.

c. Personnel requirements for maintenance of lines of communication are proportionately greater when operating in snow than under normal conditions. Manhauling or packing of ammunition in snow dissipates energy rapidly. Men must be rested, warmed, and dried periodically to keep them in a high state of efficiency. Plans for accomplishing this should be developed beforehand and adhered to in detail, otherwise attrition losses due to extreme cold will swell the casualty rate.

d. On the other hand, continued denial to the enemy of an opportunity to rest, dry out, and warm up, will swell his casualty list and result in his collapse. Warming and drying facilities should be extended to prisoners of war. Efforts should be made to apprise the enemy of the fact that prisoners may expect such facilities.

147. Objectives.

The importance of supply systems and sheltered areas increases in cold weather, and many actions will be fought to gain them for friendly use or to deny them to enemy use. The destruction of the enemy remains the paramount objective, as always, but if he can be denied supplies, shelter, and rest, the cold will accomplish his destruction with a minimum of effort on the part of friendly troops. Lines of communication are therefore primary objectives in winter warfare. These primary objectives are vulnerable to winter-trained troops and the sensitivity of the enemy to their destruction makes their rupture or destruction particularly profitable. Cutting his communication isolates the enemy, and he must attack to extricate himself. This forces him to leave his sheltered defensive system and expose himself to the cold.

148. Envelopment.

Envelopment, depending on superior oversnow mobility, is the best method of reaching enemy lines of communications. In order to be successful, the oversnow mobility of the enveloping force must be greater than that of the defending force. The necessity for a high state of training in oversnow operations thus becomes apparent, and the disadvantages imposed upon a force operating with partial training or makeshift equipment can be seen. Full use of airborne troops for the seizing of key points in rear areas should be made. The enveloping force should be composed of ski troops when possible; if they are not available, then the troops at hand having the greatest oversnow mobility for the particular type of terrain to be covered, should be used. Envelopments should start from the rear and be concealed until the last possible moment. Cold camps, night movements, and absence of motorized equipment will all be conducive to surprise. Tracks should be concealed from air observation. Wide envelopments will usually be possible because of the concentration of the enemy within defensive positions.

149. Security.

a. GENERAL. Security measures are similar to those during ordinary operations, with the addition of those which are peculiar to cold weather conditions. The silence, and in the case of ski troops, the speed with which enemy troops may move, is a factor which must always be borne in mind. When the weather permits the use of aircraft, their maximum employment may be expected.

b. ANTITANK. Antitank security will depend on evaluation of the enemy capabilities with respect to the snow conditions, vegetation, and terrain of the area. Slopes can be iced, abatis constructed, and tank traps in snow and ice and stream lines mined to supplement the limited number of antitank guns which it is possible to employ in snow. Antitank guns can be mounted on track laying oversnow vehicles for ease in transportation. This expedient allows small caliber artillery to accompany the offensive. Light antiaircraft guns will be found effective against enemy oversnow equipment.

150. Pursuit.

Ski troops should be used in the same manner as that in which cavalry or light mechanized forces are ordinarily used to maintain constant pressure on a fleeing enemy and to cut off detachments for destruction. Air operations should be continuous during pursuit because of the extreme difficulty of moving artillery forward rapidly enough to keep pace with the movement. Airborne troops may be used to seize defiles in the path of the enemy. After the enemy main force is captured or dispersed, the remnants of the enemy force should be denied all shelter and supplies in the area. The cold will then aid in the complete dissolution of the enemy forces.

Section IX. DEFENSIVE OPERATIONS

151. General.

In addition to the normal considerations which force a commander to assume the defensive, it is sometimes advisable to go on the defensive and conduct harassing operations against the enemy in an effort to force him to attack under unfavorable conditions. The defensive force, being less exposed to the cold, suffers less attrition than a force operating away from bases, and therefore conserves its strength. Harassing tactics hinder enemy operations by destruction of his lines of communication. Small offensive patrols with the mission of harassing enemy bivouacs, destroying supplies, and breaking communication routes should be dispatched for deep penetration of enemy areas. These units should be composed of men proficient in skiing or snowshoeing, woodcraft, demolition work, and tactics of small units. They should travel with the absolute minimum of equipment.

152. Reconnaissance, Selection, and Occupation of Position.

Enemy capabilities in relation to his equipment, and to the terrain, vegetation, and snow conditions of the area, should be evaluated. Reconnaissance should include reconnaissance from the direction of the enemy to insure blending of the friendly position with the background. Prior to the arrival of troops, routes to be followed in occupation of the position should be laid out and taped, and the extension of the routes to logically located dummy positions should be made in order to avoid revealing of the position by trampled snow areas. If aircraft are available to fly over the position during its occupation to report on the visibility of installations from the air, remedial action should be taken immediately on the basis of these reports.

153. Organization of Position.

a. The position should consist of mutually supporting areas capable of all-around defense.

b. Outer and inner trails should be guarded constantly by shuttling ski patrols. Patrols and messengers should use only prescribed cross trails. Broken surface of the snow at unauthorized points forms the best warning of hostile infiltration. Troops are alerted and investigation made of any trails crossing those of the prescribed network. Communication between outposts and the main body may be by radio, telephone, or pyrotechnics. Outposts should have warm shelters.

154. Obstacles.

a. WIRE. Wire entanglements installed' before snowfall may be surmounted with concertina wire, the combination being very effective. Concertina wire may be used on the surface of the snow, but danger of tunnelling under it will exist if the snow is deep. Wire as high as 12 feet to 13 feet may profitably be employed for deep snow; installation of such wire must be accomplished before snowfall.

b. OTHER OBSTACLES. Slopes may be iced to form obstacles. Pitfalls for men and tanks may be made. The ice on lakes and streams may be mined and blown as a trap and also to form an obstacle. Snow dampens the effectiveness of antitank mines. Antipersonnel mines, particularly the bounding type, are very effective, as the snow conceals the trip wires. Abatis are effective obstacles when laid on deep snow. The abatis make passage for a man wearing snow shoes or skis doubly difficult, and the deep snow delays men not wearing skis or snowshoes. The weight of the tree forces branches into the snow making tunnelling difficult. The fougasse is especially effective in frozen ground, and can be fired by a concealed trip wire.

155. Special Snow Expedients.

a. EMPLACEMENTS. Emplacements should be constructed to afford warmth for the occupants, as well as cover and concealment. Sandbags filled with snow, earth, or ice concrete may be used for their construction in deep snow or frozen ground. Loopholes and embrasures should be covered from the inside with white painted boards pushed to the front, backed up with an insulation of straw or boughs. Weapons should be sited deep within the emplacement in order to avoid muzzle blast effect. This restricts traverse and elevation, but aids in concealing the gun from sight or hearing. All emplacements must be insulated. Dummy works should be camouflaged, but not too well. Care should be taken to insure that some tracks can be seen.

b. SHELTER FOR PERSONNEL. Tunnelling in snow and the construction of trenches covered by frameworks and snow will aid in concealing positions and give shelter to personnel. In deep snow, vaulted dugouts are possible. They should be lined, when possible, to prevent cave-ins and dampness. Ventilating holes are necessary.

c. MUZZLE BLAST. Muzzle blast may be avoided by freezing a crust on the snow, by packing snow in front of the position, or by covering snow with a reversible tarpaulin white side up. These measures avoid the blowing effect of snow or minimize it; however, it will be necessary to spread new snow after firing in order to cover the discoloration produced by the muzzle blast. Hanging burlap in front of the embrasure will help to conceal muzzle blast.

Section X. RETROGRADE MOVEMENTS
156. Withdrawals.

Daylight withdrawals usually result in excessive losses and should be avoided. Protection by covering forces on the ground, and by air forces, is relatively more important in withdrawals in snow and extreme cold than during withdrawals under ordinary weather conditions. Oversnow mobility must be used to the fullest extent in order to avoid canalization. Withdrawing troops should move straight to the rear in deployed formation until beyond range of hostile small arms fire. Further withdrawal should be made in semi-deployed formations until beyond the range of hostile light artillery.

157. Delaying Action.

In addition to the usual methods of forcing deployment of the enemy when seeking to delay him, a valuable expedient is to harass enemy columns by small detachments possessing the greatest possible oversnow mobility. The poorer the enemy oversnow mobility, the greater will be the canalization of his routes, and the better the opportunity for the use of such harassing detachments. In brush or woods, the use of mortar fire will enable the detachments to bring sufficient fire on or near the enemy to force his deployment. The use of mortar fire will afford a better opportunity for escape than would be afforded had the detachment penetrated the woods to within effective small-arms range. Long-range artillery fire or air attack on enemy routes of communication are particularly valuable in snow operations.

Section XI. SPECIAL OPERATIONS

158. Attack of a Fortified Position.

a. GENERAL. Snow and extreme cold modify the attack on a fortified position by impeding or preventing the use of armored units, limiting the effectiveness of flame throwers and chemicals, slowing the advance of assault troops, and by making the transportation to the scene of action of large quantities of artillery pieces and ammunition difficult or impossible. Cutting the means of supply of the fortified enemy position, including the air supply route, and forcing the enemy to leave his fortifications and fight in the open in an attempt to break free is a desirable course of action when feasible.

b. EXPLOITATION OF BREAKTHROUGH. Ski troops and troops carried in oversnow vehicles should lead the exploitation of breakthroughs in snow and be followed by snowshoe troops for consolidation of positions.

159. Operations at River Lines.

a. GENERAL. Frozen water courses constitute avenues of approach, instead of barriers. However, open water is found even at 60° below zero and presents great dangers to personnel. Ice is not all of uniform thickness, and may be very dangerous. Streams with varying water levels are particularly dangerous, as the ice at low water will often be weaker than it appears, and will break under moderate pressure.

b. FORCING CROSSINGS. Streams should be carefully reconnoitered by engineers, who will select and make preparations for the best method of crossing. Artillery and mortar fire or aerial bombardment of ice by the enemy is an ever present probability. Troops caught on the ice by this type of enemy action are extremely vulnerable; crossing on a wide front will minimize the effects of such interference. Crossing techniques are discussed in appendix I.

c. DEFENSE AGAINST CROSSING. Dams under the control of friendly forces can be manipulated to burst the ice or to lower the water level sufficiently to reduce the bearing power of the ice cover. Ice can be mined for controlled demolition; bombardment by mortar and artillery fire or from the air may be employed. The icing of river banks is effective in hindering crossings. Traps may be built in the ice itself. In any case, the usual defense measures are necessary, as none of the means mentioned can do more than hinder a crossing.

160. Night Combat.

a. GENERAL. Night combat increases in importance in winter operations because of the relatively greater length of winter nights in general and the extreme length of such nights in high latitudes. If the surface of the snow has thawed during the day, it is apt to freeze into a crust at night, making movement easier than by day. Night operations provide concealment from hostile air reconnaissance and reduce the effectiveness of harassing bombing, and shelling, and long-range small-arms fire. The habitual use of night operations in winter campaigning is extremely probable and should be anticipated in the training period.

b. EFFECTIVENESS. If the enemy can be forced to abandon his shelters quickly while improperly clothed and to operate for a considerable time without the clothing and equipment left in his bivouac area, he will suffer numerous casualties from exposure and the morale and efficiency of his forces will be seriously impaired. Such action should be forced on him whenever possible.

161. Combat in Towns and Woods.

a. (1) The damage to shelter facilities necessitated by bombardment of a town may be avoided if infiltration into the town can be effected prior to opening the attack. Surprise must be utilized to the highest degree to prevent needless destruction.

(2) The methods described in FM 31–50 are applicable.

b. Woods, particularly if dense, form an obstacle to oversnow vehicles of all kinds. Powerful bulldozers are necessary to open roads through thick woods. Small units, equipped with necessary supporting weapons and operating under mission type orders, can be employed to advantage.

162. Mountain Warfare.

a. Units should be specially organized, trained, and equipped to operate in mountains if the double obstacles of mountainous terrain and low temperature are to be surmounted successfully. Extreme cold, coupled with the high altitudes encountered in mountain warfare, weakens men and animals and makes their work output much less than at lower altitudes and temperatures. Snow slows movement in mountains, inhibits aerial activity, and presents the dangers of avalanches. Mobile detachments capable of seizing and holding mountain heights are needed to insure movement of main bodies through the valleys.

b. For additional information on mountain warfare, see FM 70–10 (when published).

163. Combat at Defiles.

a. GENERAL. Snow in itself forms a continuous defile for organizations not having or not utilizing oversnow equipment; it also increases the effectiveness of woods or rough terrain as obstacles to cross-country progress. In deploying from columns, oversnow equipment should be regarded as the means for utilizing the entire snow surface as a potential road, rather than an obstacle.

b. OFFENSIVE AGAINST DEFILES. Full utilization of oversnow mobility should be made to envelop defiles. Defiles should be seized as far as practicable in advance of the main body, using light forces, extremely mobile equipment, and boldness. Airborne troops are suitable for advance seizure of defiles.

c. DEFENSE OF DEFILES. The reserve of a defensive force at a defile must be extremely mobile in order to counter any envelopments attempted by the enemy. Flank outposts should be established and should be in communication with the reserve. If no delaying action is contemplated, the holding force at the defile may be deprived of oversnow equipment to augment the mobility of the reserve.

164. Partisan Warfare.

a. Partisan warfare against enemy supply and communication lines is especially valuable in operations in snow and extreme cold. Hunters and trappers are ideal partisans in sparsely settled country.

b. For more complete discussion, see FM 100–5.

Section XII. AIRBORNE OPERATIONS

165. General.

a. Airborne troops should be employed wherever and whenever possible because the snow does not limit their strategic mobility, as it does that of ground troops. They should be used to seize and hold key points until the slower moving ground troops can arrive.

b. For employment of airborne troops, see FM 71–30.

166. Parachute Troops.

Individual oversnow equipment should accompany jumpers. If, in snow-covered areas, snowshoes and skis are dropped separately by parachute, the men will be immobilized for a considerable length of time. In deep snow, they will be almost helpless. Organizational oversnow equipment can be dropped separately.

167. Plane and Glider Transported Troops.

If troops are transported by plane, the clearing and compacting of snow runways must be accomplished before landing is possible. This may be done by parachute or glider-borne troops. Glider and plane transported troops must have individual snow crossing equipment loaded in the same plane or glider in which they ride.

Section XIII. SUPPLY AND EVACUATION

168. Method of Supply.

Oversnow equipment must be used for forward supply, augmented by manhauling and animal transport where necessary. Tractor and sled trains should be organized. These trains can be used for transport of heavy supplies in areas having no road net. Organization and training must be complete before beginning operations, as attempts to operate special equipment with inexperienced crews is wasteful and relatively ineffective. Motor fuel consumption will increase over normal due to incomplete combustion, idling of engines, and a proportionately greater amount of low gear driving. An increase in the amount of explosives needed should be anticipated. Ration increases of 50 percent to cover losses in dropping, increased consumption, and spoiling should also be anticipated. Air supply should be used when appropriate.

169. Ammunition.

Ammunition should be stored above the ground and kept covered. It should be carefully cleaned of ice and frozen earth with a wooden tool before use.

170. Evacuation of Wounded.

a. GENERAL. Wounded men often freeze to death unless promptly cared for or if they have lost their sleeping bags. To prevent a large percentage of deaths among the wounded in extremely cold weather, it is necessary to insure their prompt collection on the battlefield, and their speedy evacuation to places where they can be kept warm. To this end, the size of collecting parties will have to be increased above normal requirements and they must be provided with enclosed sleds equipped with heating devices. Advance planning is necessary to provide adequate evacuation methods in snow and cold. Cold hastens the progress of shock and lessens the chances of recovery if the casualty is exposed to it for any length of time. Enemy action hinders the use of litters in snow, as bearers in sufficient number to carry the litter become a good group target.

b. METHODS OF EVACUATION. Litters are difficult to handle in deep snow, but small sleds and toboggans provide an excellent means of collecting the disabled. Sleeping bags or casualty evacuation bags must be on hand in ample numbers so that wounded men can be kept warm. Heated shelter should be provided frequently along the route of evacuation at which warm fluid such as cocoa or soup is administered. Dressings also should be checked and shock therapy administered if necessary. Drinking water for the wounded should be warmed. Ambulances should be heated and provided with warm bedding. Ambulance planes should be readily available for the speedy evacuation of serious cases. The akja, shown in figure 19, may be drawn by one or by two men crawling in tandem using the harness shown, and in snow operations should be made up in sufficient quantities to replace litters completely. A small movable house built to fit a truck body or cargo sled will provide adequate temporary shelter and warmth for the wounded. Issue toboggans are useful for evacuation. The mountain tent or the shelter half may be used with the wounded man's snowshoes or skis to form an improvised toboggan.

171. Care of Wounded or Frozen.

a. GENERAL. Wounded men should be warmed by every possible means. Heated bricks or stones wrapped in burlap may be inserted in sleeping bags, warm nonalcoholic drinks administered, shelters utilized, and speedy evacuation to the rear effected.

b. THAWING. To thaw frozen members, keep the member cold. Warm the individual by hot non-alcoholic drinks, heated pads, coverings. Massage the body between the trunk and the frozen member, taking care not to touch the frozen area. In this manner, circulation is restored at the same time the member thaws from within, and damage to tissue is held to a minimum. Warming the member thaws it without restoration of circulation and causes death of tissues so thawed with corresponding sloughing of parts and probable loss of the member.

Appendix I

COLD WEATHER FIELD ENGINEERING EXPEDIENTS

Section I. STREAM CROSSING

1. General.

a. Contrary to general opinion, not all streams freeze over in extremely low temperature. Streams may have open water or very thin ice in temperatures as low as 60° below zero. Frozen lakes and water courses may be turned into obstacles by rupturing the ice by explosives. This may be effected by mines, artillery fire, mortar fire, or air bombing, and secures the best results when done immediately before the arrival of hostile troops. Overflows are often encountered in low temperatures due to natural causes, but they can also be caused by manipulation of dams. Water is one of the most dangerous types of obstacles at low temperatures, as wet feet will freeze unless all wet footgear is at once removed, feet dried, and dry footgear put on.

b. For more complete discussion of stream-crossing expedients see FM 5–10.

c. A part of the supporting value of ice is derived from its pressure on the water below it. When the water level falls, the bearing capacity of the ice decreases. In extreme cold, streams often have layers of ice interspersed with layers of running water. In any crossing of ice, reconnaissance of the ice is necessary to insure that its bearing quality is adequate, and that men and animals will not wet their feet. Rotten ice can be detected by its dull color and honeycombed structure. It has very little supporting power. In judging ice thickness, the layers of rotten ice on top and bottom should not be considered. Sample blocks should be cut or thickness at the crossing site measured. In general, troops crossing ice should not halt nor should vehicles turn around thereon. Traffic onto the ice should be controlled.

d. The following table may be used as a guide to determine what weight can be supported by ice of varying thicknesses and at what interval between columns:

TABLE OF LOADS ON ICE

Load	Thickness of ice	Minimum width of track or interval
	Inches	Feet
Single rifleman on skis or snowshoes..	1½	16
Infantry in single file, 2-pace distance	3	23
Infantry columns, single horses, motorcycles, unloaded sleds or motor toboggans.....................	4	33
Single light artillery piece. ¼-ton truck 4 x 4.....................	6	49
Light artillery, passenger cars, medium 1½-ton trucks with total load of 3½ tons....................	8	65
2½-ton trucks, light loads..........	10	82
Closed columns of all arms except armored force and heavy artillery.	12	98
Armored scout cars, light tanks......	14	115
20-ton vehicles....................	16	131
45-ton vehicles....................	24	164

2. Ice Bridges.

a. GENERAL. Ice bridges may be used to cross open channels in a slow-moving stream. The ice used must be consistent in thickness and quality; no obstacle should exist in the channel on either bank; the ice should be thick enough to support the load, or strengthened; and cutting should be accurately done to insure a close fit at either end.

b. Figures 27 and 28 illustrate skew and straight ice bridges. The skew bridge is the easier to construct as accurate survey and cutting to insure a close joint are less necessary than for the straight bridge.

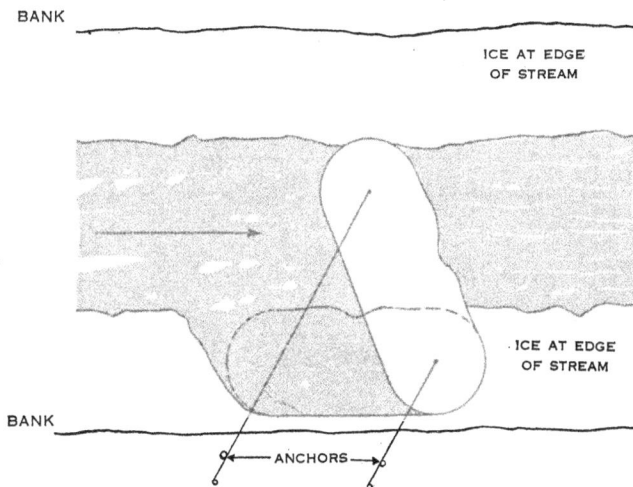

Figure 27. Skew ice bridge.

c. BRIDGING FROM BOTH BANKS. If the bank ice is very irregular or the span to be crossed very large, it may be necessary to cut and swing out ice blocks from both banks.

d. REINFORCING ICE. The simplest method of reinforcing ice is to put layers of snow and small lumps of ice on the surface and pour on water to freeze; each layer should be frozen before addition of the subsequent layer. Another method of increasing the carrying capacity of the ice is by adding and freezing to it several layers of boughs or straw, each about 2 inches to 4 inches thick. Boards, planks, and small logs may be used to form tracks

137

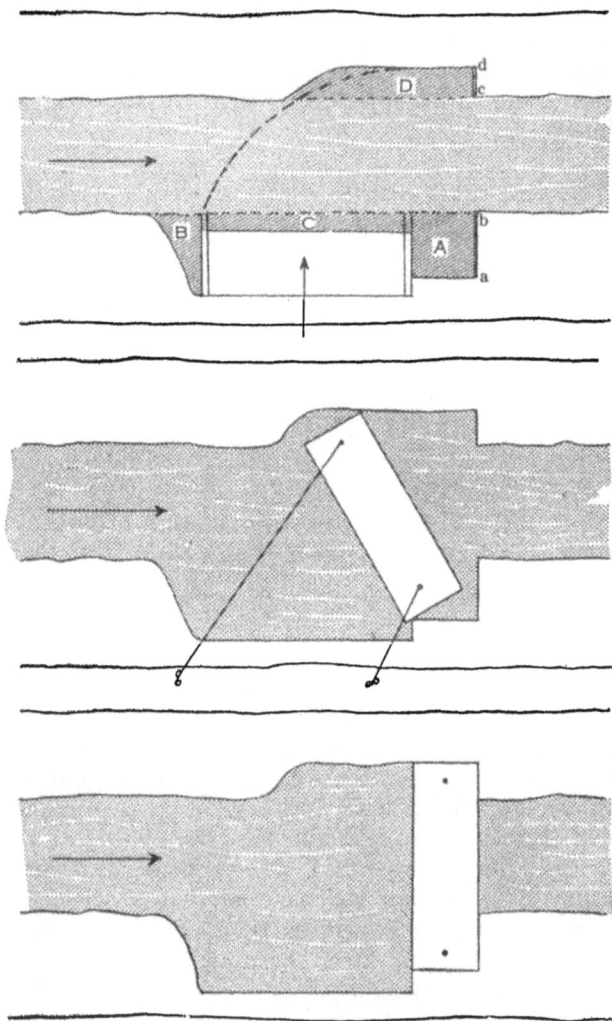

Figure 28. Straight ice bridge.

or runways for wheels or runners. Each track should be at least 3 feet wide. Sleds made of logs will help in distributing the load of artillery pieces. The following table may be used as a guide in the reinforcement of ice:

ICE REINFORCEMENT TABLE

Material	Thickness of reinforcing layer	Required for 13 foot wide track	Increase in bearing capacity (assuming ice thickness of 6 inches)
Ice and snow	3 layers of 1½ inches.	————	⅛
Straw.......	2 to 4 inches	6 pounds per foot run.	⅛
Straw, 3.....	Each layer 2 to 4 inches.	20 pounds per foot run.	¼
Brush.......	2 to 4 inches.	2 cubic feet per foot run.	¼
Ice block....	Dependent on size of blocks.	————	————
Planks, 2-inch	————	Two runways, each 3 feet wide.	½

e. Ponton Bridges. (1) Many times it will be quicker to blow up weak surface ice and use normal ponton equipment. Enemy action also may necessitate this type of crossing. All boats and pontons should be protected by rubbing strakes of sheet metal to prevent their being punctured by the ice. Chopping of the ice around the pontons frequently will be necessary to prevent crushing of the pontons. Pontons may also be protected by floats or booms on the upstream side. Ice breakers should be installed upstream (fig. 29). Anchor cables should be protected by wooden casings at water level. Men on the pontons should fend off floes with boat hooks. Large floes should be destroyed upstream by explosives placed by boat parties. Floes greater than 20 feet square make ponton bridging almost impossible.

(2) When floes make ponton bridging impossible, cable crossings may be used.

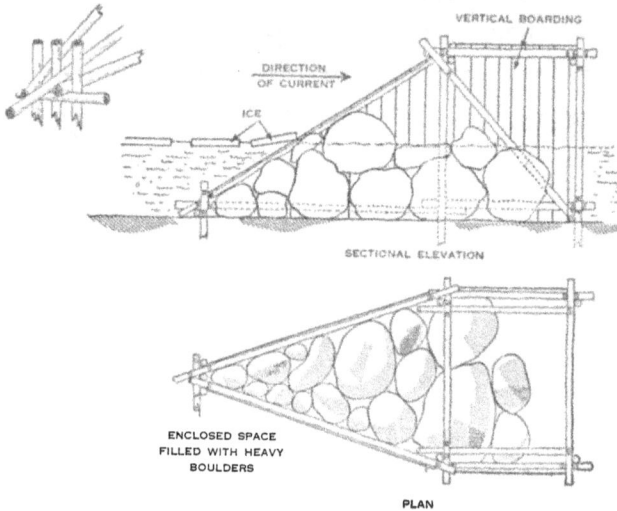

Figure 29. Ice breakers.

f. FORDING AND TESTING BY TRACTOR. If streams are known to be relatively shallow, and if the bed is sloping and comparatively firm, caterpillar tractors may be used to test the bearing capacity of ice. The engine exhaust stack and other vents are prolonged to a height in excess of water level when the tractor is on the bottom. Wire cables, harnessed to anchor tractors on the shore, are attached to the tractor before it is sent on the ice. The caterpillar is then started slowly across the ice. If it should break through, and the water is so deep that it cannot climb the far bank, the cables harnessed to the anchor tractors can haul it back. Personnel should not ride on the tractor. Frequently ice may be tested in this way more quickly than in any other.

g. SALVAGE AND RESCUE DETAILS. Salvage and rescue details should be formed and posted before any attempts at crossings are made. In addition to being prepared to recover personnel and equipment, members of these details can be used for traffic control.

Section II. SHELTERS AND FIELD WORKS

3. Ice Concrete.

Ice concrete is an easily prepared effective reinforcement for shelters and emplacements. It consists of a mixture of sand and water, or sand, gravel, and water frozen solid, and is stronger than ordinary ice. A layer of earth or moss over ice concrete prevents thawing. Ice concrete is made by slowly mixing water and sand (and gravel, if used) in a trough. The mixture is applied in layers which must be firmly frozen before the addition of subsequent layers. Because of the dangers incident to thawing, dugouts constructed of ice concrete must be especially marked.

4. Snow and Ice Protection Against Enemy Fire.

The depth of the snow will determine whether emplacements should be built by excavation, excavation and breastworks, or breastworks alone. The protective value of snow and ice against shell splinters and small arms fire is shown below:

Type	Minimum thickness for protection
	Feet
Newly fallen snow..............	18
Firmly frozen snow............	12
Packed snow...................	7 to 8
Ice...........................	3½

5. Sandbag.

If it is impossible to dig in because of frozen ground, deep snow, lack of time, or the necessity for silence, cover above ground level may be obtained by stacking sandbags and pouring water over them. The outside should be plastered with packed snow. Loose snow should be added for camouflage. Bags may be filled with snow reinforced by ice concrete.

6. Logs.

Positions for one or two riflemen, an automatic rifle team or machine gun crew may be built of logs or railroad ties. The logs are stacked and fastened to form an open square. The firing slit is just above the snow surface. The positions are built into the snow and covered with packed snow if roofed. If not roofed, they must be covered with white cloth or by shelter halves covered with snow. Firing slits are closed by boards painted white on the side toward the enemy. The open side should be covered with an angled cover of white. Roof cover of an easily removable type for the front portion at least is necessary if mortars are to be fired or if crews of weapons are to defend themselves with hand grenades.

7. Earthworks.

If possible, earthworks should be constructed before the ground is frozen. In locating embrasures, the probable average depth of the snow should be considered. If it is impossible to construct earthworks before the freezing period, the ground may be sufficiently thawed by mobile steam generators to make holes into which explosives can be inserted for blasting. If time is available, the mobile steam generator and tube assembly can thaw the ground sufficiently to permit excavation with ordinary tools. Air compressors and concrete breakers can be used in hard frozen soil to good effect. If materials are available steam points can be improvised by mounting a small steam boiler on a chassis or sled, and adjusting the live steam outlet to a manifold connected by hoses to perforated metal pipes whose lower ends are pointed. The hot pipes are pushed down into the frozen earth about 5 feet and live steam turned on. The area is covered by a tarpaulin. Complete thawing depends on the distances which the pipes penetrate below the frost line; good results, however, may be obtained in permanently frozen ground. Sandy soil is the easiest to thaw by this method.

8. Tunnelling and Covered Works.

All communication trenches should have snow covers or be tunnelled through thes now. Lattice work laid over the trench and covered with flat

Figure 30. Lattice and snow-covered trenches.

143

snow blocks which are in turn covered with powdery snow are shown in figure 30. Snow tunnelling and snow covered emplacements are measures essential to camouflage of positions, for even after positions are discovered, the enemy will find it difficult to adjust his fire.

9. Positions of Automatic Weapons.

Automatic weapons, with limited traverse and elevation, may be concealed by placing them toward the rear of the emplacement so that the muzzle blast is concealed within the emplacement. When weapons are so placed, the top course of sandbags should not be frozen to the rest of the emplacement, as this course may have to be shifted in order to permit fire at wider traverse and greater elevations. Shifting may also be desirable in order to use alternate slits.

10. Construction of Field Works and Shelters.

In the construction of field works and shelters, several times the normal amount of time for construction of works must be allotted because of the difficulty of working frozen ground and the lessened working capacity of men in extreme cold. In addition, the need for special equipment such as compressed air concrete breakers and portable thawing boilers and points must be anticipated. For speedy and silent construction, cloth sandbags may be filled in the rear areas. After they have been placed, water should be poured over them and snow packed on them while freezing. When not in the presence of the enemy, earthworks may be constructed by clearing and piling snow, then cutting furrows in the frozen ground with picks and undercutting sections between furrows. These sections can be lifted out. Concrete breakers may be used to expedite the work. Bulldozers may be employed, once the crust is broken. In deep snow, emplacements should be partially above snow level. Embrasures and loopholes must be above this level.

11. Drainage.

Drainage must be carefully considered in siting all installations, as unseasonable thaws are likely to occur, followed by cold weather. If men and equipment get wet during the thaw they will be incapacitated by the cold. When the spring thaws commence, emplacements must be usable until new ones are constructed; construction must commence promptly, as melting of the snow reveals emplacements which have been hidden during freezing weather.

12. Road Blocks.

Road blocks (fig. 31) may be made by icing drifts and roads, and by the use of ice concrete and wire cable. A cable block consists of a piece of 1-inch wire cable stretched diagonally across the road about 2 feet above the surface at or near a fill or on a hill. It is most effective if placed so that it is approached by vehicles coming down hill. Anti-tank mines may be placed in the ditch toward which the vehicle is deflected. This type of block has the advantage of being easy to construct, is difficult to detect, and is readily removable for the passage of friendly vehicles or troops. Effectiveness of the block is increased by icing the road on either side of the cable. Stretching the cable diagonally causes vehicles to be deflected into ditches.

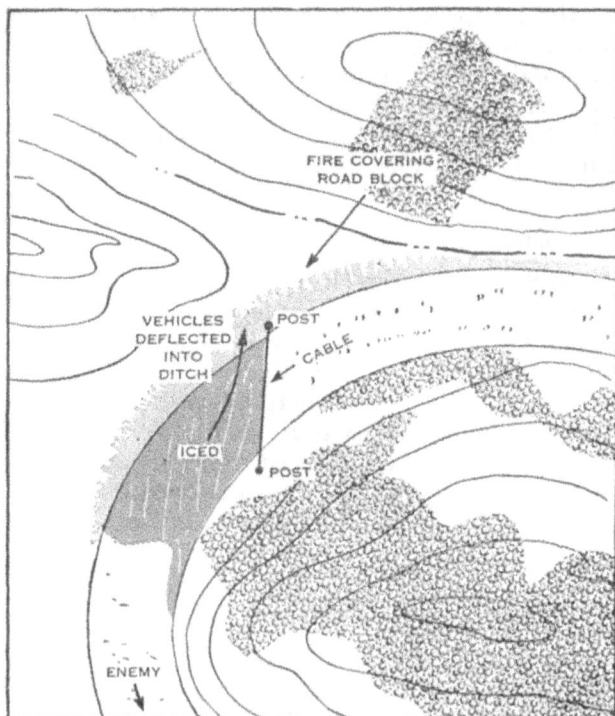

Figure 31. Road block.

13. Wire.

Wire entanglements should be placed so that snow will not drift completely over them, otherwise they can be crossed by men on snowshoes. When it is impossible to screw the issue iron pickets into frozen ground, poles made into trestles can be substituted. Wire obstructions, requiring no posts, such as chevaux-de-frise, loops, and cylinders (concertinas), are often effective. In deep snow wire must be erected on especially high pickets. In woods it can

146

be attached to trees. High wire entanglement should be erected before snowfall if possible.

14. Fougasse.

When a fougasse is to be installed in an avenue of approach, the earth trench can best be constructed by concrete breakers as the resulting clods are more suitable as projectiles than earth broken by hand. The effectiveness of the fougasse is increased in frozen ground, but diminished by heavy snowfall. Snow may, however, be used effectively to mask the trip wire. Care should be taken not to bury the trip wire so deeply that it is ineffective.

15. Antipersonnel Mines.

Antipersonnel mines are easy to conceal in snow. They may be placed in barbed wire obstacles, and hung so that they will be just covered by the snow. The trip wires may be attached to a strand of barbed wire in such a way that anyone hitting that strand fires the fuze. In all installations the mine should be placed where it is covered with the smallest possible amount of snow. In shallow snow, the trip wires may be concealed in the snow. In deep snow, they must be above snow level, as the enemy will be using snowshoes or skis.

16. Antitank Mines.

Minefields should be laid before or during a snow storm as falling snow is the only certain conceal-ment of the field. Mines laid in roads or tracks where the snow is already disturbed may arouse no suspicion. Antitank mines must be placed on a solid surface to insure that they will be detonated when the tank tread rolls over them. A hole may be dug in the snow down to the frozen ground surface and the mine placed, or, if the snow is deep, an excavation can be made, a plank inserted, and the mine laid on the plank as a base. In either case, the mine is covered with snow.

17. Woods and Abatis.

a. Snow, combined with thick woods and fallen trees or underbrush, forms an obstacle to all vehicular traffic. Woods must, however, be considered as likely avenues of approach for small mobile ski and snowshoe units. The abatis is very effective in deep snow against ski and snowshoe troops, as well as vehicles. Abatis road blocks can be readily constructed by using the bulldozer to pull over large trees. Barbed wire is then interlaced in the abatis to make its removal more difficult.

b. Trip mines adjusted to explode when an attempt is made to clear the road, are easily concealed in such blocks. (See FM 5–15.)

c. Deciduous trees make the best abatis. A deciduous abatis forces snowshoe and ski troops to remove their snowshoes or skis and the deep snow then acts as an additional obstacle. Coniferous trees are less suitable because the boughs provide matting and minimize the tangling effect, making crossing while wearing snowshoes and skis easier.

d. Abatis should be sited so they cannot easily be by-passed. They may be penetrated by the use of bangalore torpedoes or crossed by the use of coverings of chicken wire or matting.

18. Antitank Obstacles.

a. Ice may be utilized to form an effective tank trap. Figure 32 illustrates the construction and insulation of such a trap.

(1) The marking out of the trap and removal of snow from the ice is shown in ① . The line of

the channel of the stream (or the deep portion of the lake) is marked out, snow is cleared, and a strip of ice sawed out by parallel cuts one foot apart. At least one saw cut must incline away from the center. This enables the strip to be removed by depressing one side and forcing it under the lip.

(2) The method of sawing the block and tilting it for removal is shown in ② . To prevent refreezing of the channel and to conceal the obstacle, an insulating mat supported on light lath frames is placed between the two banks.

(3) The placing of the frames and the unrolling of the insulating mats over them is shown in ③ .

(4) The replacement of the snow is shown in ④ . This obstacle is best constructed in early winter while the ice is still thin, although sometimes there may not be enough snow at this time of year to provide adequate insulation and concealment. Ice less than 8 inches thick cannot be used for this type of trap. Toward the end of the winter when further hard freezing is infrequent the mats may be removed. The forming of new ice makes the trap an effective antipersonnel obstacle provided the thickness of the new ice does not exceed 2 inches.

(5) The ends of the frames are placed in recesses in the ice and packed with snow on ice chips. The frames will soon freeze to the ice. Frames are placed at intervals of 1 foot 6 inches to 2 feet. The mats are normally 15 to 16 feet long and 4 to 5 feet wide. Each mat should be supported on three frames. The snow cover should be 4 to 6 inches thick, and should be always maintained at that thickness as a channel covered by mats alone without snow insulation will refreeze very quickly. This obstacle should remain effective for a period of six weeks to two months.

149

① MARKING TRAP AND REMOVING SNOW

② SAWING AND TILTING BLOCK.

③ INSULATING COVER IN PLACE.

④ COVER CAMOUFLAGED BY SNOW.

⑤ DETAILS OF CONSTRUCTION
OF INSULATING MATS

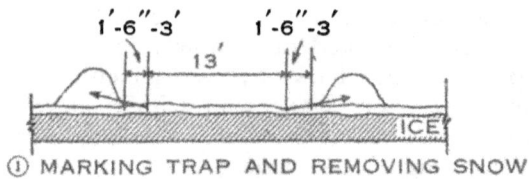

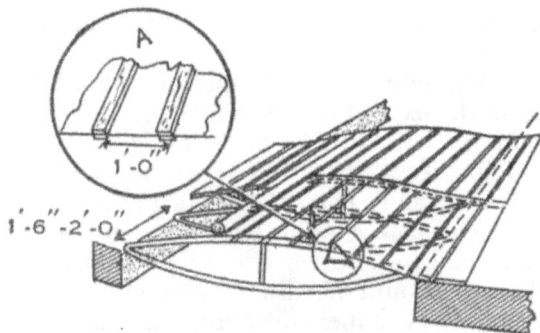

Figure 32. Water tank trap.

b. Antitank ditches may be camouflaged to resemble ordinary trenches.

c. Successive banks of lightly packed snow are frequently effective as antitank obstacles.

19. Demolitions.

Explosives do not freeze at moderately low temperatures; they do, however, freeze at temperatures below 20° below zero. Dynamite freezes below 20° below zero and is not dependable at low temperatures. Caps should not be inserted in the jacket, but should be taped to the outside. TNT is very little affected by low temperature. Fuzes burn more slowly at low temperatures. (See also FM 5–25.) Explosives should be kept in storage in temperatures above zero and should not be exposed to the cold for a longer time than necessary before using.

20. Camouflage.

For information on camouflage, see FM 5–20, 5–20A to 5–20H, and TM 5–267 and supplements.

21. Water Supply.

a. GENERAL. The need for a large amount of water, though not immediately apparent, becomes pronounced in men operating in the cold after the first two or three days. This need is intensified by the consumption of concentrated and dehydrated food, and by the evaporation of moisture from the body by the dry air characteristic of most localities when the temperature is lower than 30° below zero. Water may be obtained from running streams, by fuel or solar melting of snow or ice, and by pumping. It must be remembered that water thus obtained is not necessarily free from contamination; appropriate steps must always be taken for its decontamination.

b. Pumping Water. Water may be pumped from holes chopped through the ice. It is desirable, if practicable, to improvise heaters to prevent freezing of the pump. Pumps not equipped with heaters should be thawed with hot water and packed with straw inside wooden outer jackets.

22. Water from Snow and Ice.

a. By Solar Thawing. (1) Dark colored surfaces absorb heat, while light colored ones reflect it. Small patches of snow placed in strong sunlight on a background of dark water-repellent material will melt and can be collected. A shelter half, patches of dark rock or pavement may be used. Care must be taken that too much snow is not placed on the dark surface at one time, or it will not melt.

(2) When temperatures are sufficiently high, a conical well may be dug in deep snow and water formed by melting snow collected at the bottom.

b. By Heated Container. See paragraph 6.

Section III. IGLOOS

23. General.

a. The Eskimo type of igloo is a very useful shelter and can be built easily if the snow is deep enough and of the right consistency. However, its construction requires practice and familiarity with snow as a material. It is especially valuable in treeless, uninhabited areas, or when tents are not available.

b. The igloo is a domed house made of snow blocks. It offers protection against wind and cold and partial protection against small arms fire and shell fragments. It can be occupied throughout the winter.

c. There are several methods of construction, one of which is described in this manual.

d. The igloo can accommodate from 2 to 50 men, depending on its size. For a short stay, a small igloo is preferable; for a long stay, a large one. If the snow is of poor quality, several small igloos can be built more quickly than one large one. One typical igloo has a diameter of 16 feet, measured through the thickness of the snow blocks, and an interior diameter of 12 feet 8 inches. It is 7 feet high inside. The walls are 20 inches thick, not including the snow piled around the outside. It has proved to be especially practical as a shelter for 12 men.

24. Building Equipment.

The equipment desirable for the construction of igloos consists of the following: saws and large knives for cutting and trimming snowblocks; shovels for packing snow; hatchets for cutting ice; a wooden form (trapezoid shape) for measuring snow blocks; a piece of string, 10 feet long, for use as a radius string.

25. Condition of Snow.

Dry, hard snow, from which snow blocks can be cut quickly, is best suited for building an igloo. Frozen snow is less suitable; fresh powdery snow is useless. The thickness and solidity of the snow are tested by probing. Suitable snow should be at least 12 inches thick. The lower layers under powdery snow may be cut into blocks after the loose snow is removed. Thawing snow can always be used. If the snow is not deep, large snow balls can be made by rolling; blocks are then cut out. The thicker the blocks, the more quickly the building will be finished.

153

26. Preparation for Building.

A center point is fixed by driving an intrenching tool or a wooden peg into the ground or snow. The measuring line (radius string) is tied to the tool or peg in the center at snow level. It remains so fastened while in use. For an igloo of 16-foot diameter, knots are tied in the string at 6 feet 4 inches (interior radius) and 8 feet (exterior radius) and circles inscribed on the surface. The foundation is laid between the two concentric circles.

27. Cutting the Blocks.

The snow blocks are cut out of a pit with vertical walls 12 to 20 inches long. The site of the igloo itself may provide some of the blocks. Standing in the pit, a man cuts out blocks along the edge of the pit in order to obtain perpendicular rather than slanting surfaces. It is advisable, especially for beginners, to use a wooden form of trapezoidal shape (fig. 33). In cutting the blocks, the long and the short parallel sides are alternately placed on the edge of the pit. The resulting pattern is shown in

Figure 33. Cutting blocks using form.

figure 34. The blocks should be lifted out carefully to avoid damaging their surfaces. The speed of building depends primarily on the speed with which the blocks can be cut. Therefore, the men charged with this task must be relieved frequently.

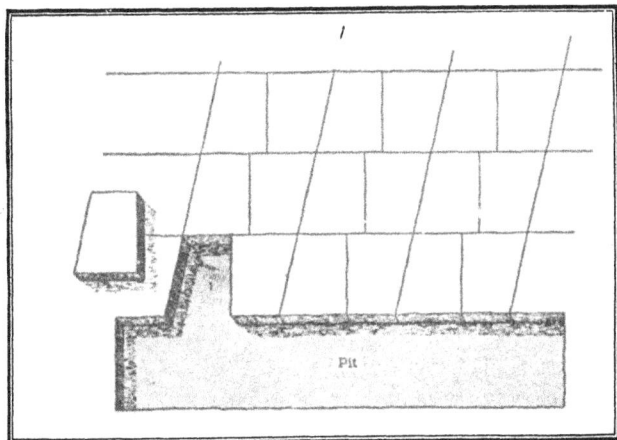

Figure 34. Block patterns.

28. Building the First Tier.

The blocks are fitted together within the double lines of the two circles. The surfaces marked "a" which are 13 inches long, face inside (fig. 35); the surfaces marked "b" which are 16 inches long, face outside. The thickness of the wall (marked "c") is 20 inches. The block is slanted slightly inward by undercutting the underside. The degree of slant can be determined by using the radius string, extending it to outer edge of wall, and shaving off the snow on the under side of the block so that the string is one straight line to the outer edge. Blocks should be placed so that the outer edges are no greater distance from center stake than the outer knot on the string.

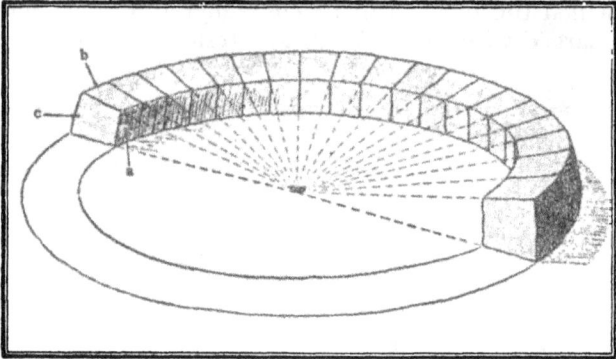

Figure 35. Placing of blocks.

29. Building the Second and Successive Tiers.

The second tier (fig. 36) can be started·at any place. The third block to the left of the starting point is shaved off until approximately the upper quarter is removed; the upper half of the second block is then removed and three quarters of the first block. These three blocks are shaved to a continuous slope. The first block in the second tier is placed in the niche formed by the last full block and the quarter block on its left. The second tier and successive tiers are built to the left and the entire igloo is made in a continuous ascending spiral. For left-handed builders, all these steps are reversed and the spiral is built to the right.

30. Completing the Dome.

When the house is all but completed, the center of the dome overhead is a small irregular space. A block somewhat larger than this space is cut, set on

Figure 36. Construction of igloo.

end and lifted vertically through the hole, and
lowered to a horizontal position on top of the
opening. The opening and the block are then
trimmed to size and the block, or keystone, drops
into place. It is important to cut and fit this block
carefully as it keeps the others from falling.

31. Tunnel.

An S-shaped tunnel (fig. 37) 10 to 13 feet long,
about 2 feet wide, and 4 feet high, may be added to
the entrance. The side walls of the tunnel consist
of rectangular blocks. The ceiling consists of snow
blocks placed either horizontally or in an inverted
V-shape. The S-form of the tunnel provides protection against wind. In deep snow, this tunnel may
be below the surface of the snow. At the point
where the tunnel joins the igloo, it can be enlarged
sufficiently to form a large anteroom (a small igloo,
about 6 feet in diameter). The anteroom serves as
a storeroom and as a place for removing the snow
from the clothing before entering the igloo.

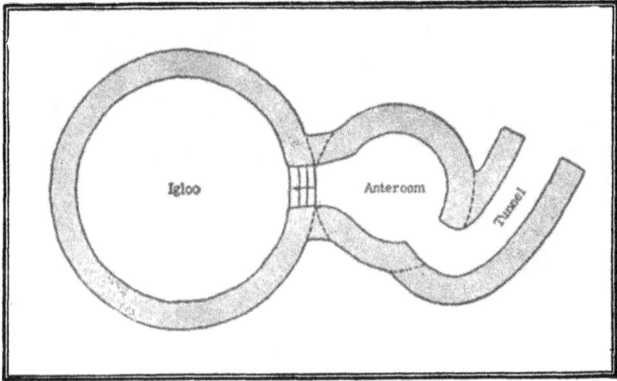

Figure 37. Igloo showing anteroom and tunnel.

32. Finishing Touches.

There will be crevices between blocks which must be chinked with soft snow. Blocks protruding on the inside are smoothed down. The outside of the igloo is left rough to provide a holding surface for a cover of snow which will fill in the cracks and further strengthen the structure. The snow cover is made to serve a double purpose around the lower part of the igloo. Banked to a thickness of 10 feet or more, the snow helps to provide protection against rifle fire and shell fragments. It also camouflages the igloo to make it resemble a snowdrift. A ventilation hole is made in the roof. Holes may be cut into the wall to admit light.

33. Furnishings.

About two-thirds of the floor space should be a sleeping platform, made of snow blocks. The platform and the floor of the igloo should be covered with insulating materials. Branches of birch, willow, larch, fir, Scotch pine, dry leaves, underbrush,

158

boards, heather, dry moss, hay, straw, paper, cardboard, animal skins, shelter halves, woolen blankets, sleds, and skis are suitable. Layers with plenty of air space between them are excellent (for instance, alternate layers of shelter halves and brushwood).

34. Heating.

The newly built igloo should be heated by cooking apparatus, kerosene lamps, candles, or similar heating equipment, until the snow is thawed almost to the slush point. The source of heat is then shut off, and the igloo freezes, the inside surface being glazed with ice. This glaze strengthens the house and gives it a smooth finish inside so that melting snow will not drip but will run along the walls. Before retiring at night, the occupants of the igloo must extinguish all fires and close the entrance at the outer end of the tunnel with snow blocks.

Appendix II
SKIING

Section I. PHYSICAL TRAINING

1. General.

Skiing uses many muscles which are not ordinarily used in the field or in the usual physical training, and therefore causes stiffness in those muscles during the early stages of ski training. Beginners also have a tendency to stiffen up so that they fall with tense muscles. To offset these conditions, ski conditioning exercises and snow tumbling together with appropriate exercises described in FM 21-20 comprise the initial phase of ski training. They are continued during the advanced phases of the training.

2. Ski Conditioning Exercises.

The following exercises are useful for ski conditioning:

a. ANKLE EXERCISE. Starting position: side straddle position, (feet parallel, 30 inches apart on the ground) hands on hips. Roll the feet outward on ONE; recover on TWO; roll to the inside of the feet on THREE; recover on FOUR. The knees are relaxed and on the count of THREE should be allowed to bend as far forward as they go, heels on the ground. Cadence, slow.

b. COMBINED TRUNK BENDING AND TWISTING EXERCISE. Starting position: side straddle position, (feet parallel, 30 inches apart, heels on ground) arms sideward. Twist trunk one-quarter turn to the right on ONE; bend down at the waist while remaining twisted to the right on TWO; rise, but remain twisted to the right on THREE; recover on FOUR. Alternate exercise from right to left. Cadence, moderate.

c. KNEE BENDING EXERCISE. Starting position: Side straddle position, (feet parallel, 6 inches apart, heels on ground) hands on hips. Quarter knee bend on ONE; half knee bend on TWO; full knee bend, arms forward on THREE; recover on FOUR. Cadence, slow, rising rapidly on fourth count. On every second exercise, rise slowly on the fourth count.

d. BALANCING EXERCISE. Starting position: Attention. Arms and trunk extended to a forward horizontal position, with right leg extended to the rear on ONE; bend left knee as much as possible on TWO; straighten knee on THREE; recover on FOUR. Alternate exercise from right to left. Cadence slow.

e. CHEST AND SHOULDER EXERCISE. Starting position: Attention, arms at the horizontal flex. Snap elbows to the rear on ONE; repeat on TWO; repeat on THREE; arms extended and stretched on the extreme rear on FOUR. Recover after each count. Cadence, moderate.

f. COMBINED BALANCING AND STRETCHING EXERCISE. Starting position: Attention. Arms and right leg extending forward to a horizontal position on ONE; arms overhead and right leg backwards with snap on TWO; return to position of one on THREE; recover on FOUR. Alternate exercise from right to left. Cadence, slow to moderate.

g. ANKLE EXERCISE. Starting position: Hands on hips. Right leg extended and raised 18 inches from the ground, toe pointed on ONE; toe raised toward knee on TWO; return to position of one on THREE; recover on FOUR. Alternate to the left leg, after sufficiently exercising right leg. Cadence, moderate to fast.

h. LEG EXERCISE. Starting position: Side straddle position, (feet parallel and 36 inches apart, heels on ground) arms sideward. Right knee fully bent with left leg straight and both feet flat on the ground on ONE; recover on TWO; to the left on THREE; recover on FOUR. The trunk is held erect throughout exercise. Cadence, slow to moderate.

i. LEG EXERCISE. Starting position: Hands on hips, left foot placed 18 inches in front of right, knees fully bent, heels flat on ground, trunk erect, weight equally distributed on both feet. Positions of the feet are alternated with a hop on ONE; recover on TWO. Cadence, moderate to fast.

j. TRUNK-TWISTING EXERCISE. Starting position: Side straddle position, (feet 20 inches apart, heels on the ground) arms to the thrust, knees bent. Twist sharply to the right on ONE; recover on TWO; full twist to the left on THREE; recover on FOUR. Elbows kept stiff throughout the exercise. Cadence, moderate to fast.

k. CROUCHING EXERCISE. Starting position: Side straddle position, (feet parallel and 20 inches apart, heels on ground) low crouch, hands on knees. Force knees together on ONE; apart on TWO. Elbows kept stiff throughout the exercise as heels remain on the ground. Cadence, slow to moderate.

3. Snow Tumbling.

Snow tumbling, designed to limber the muscles, teach relaxation in falling, and instill self-confidence, is similar to that on ordinary ground. The forward, right forward, left forward, and back roll should be employed. It is desirable to have tumbling experience at the beginning of each day's exercise.

Section II. SKI DRILL

4. General.

Ski drill is commenced as soon as the soldier has received sufficient training in elementary skiing to assume the positions and execute the various elements of the drill. Ski drill and training in elementary skiing should be given concurrently. The terrain and climate in which ski troops will operate require that normal ski drill be reduced to the minimum necessary for assembly, organization, instruction, and speedy reaction to commands. All infantry drill movements (FM 22–5) that are easily performed on skis are used. In addition, the following are prescribed.

5. Positions.

a. ATTENTION (fig. 38). (1) Skis being in the hand: See Order Skis (par. 7*a*).

(2) Skis being mounted: Skis are parallel, bindings touching; poles, grasped properly are so placed ` that points are on line with and three inches outside toes of boots. Elbows are close to the side; forearms horizontal.

b. FALLING IN. At the command FALL IN, the squad forms as prescribed in FM 22–5.

(1) Skis being in the hand: Normal interval (40 inches) will be taken.

(2) Skis being mounted: Ski interval will be taken. This is approximately 9 feet, and is measured by extending the right arm and ski pole and the left arm, on which the left pole hangs from the wrist.

c. AT EASE. (1) Skis being in the hand: Same as

163

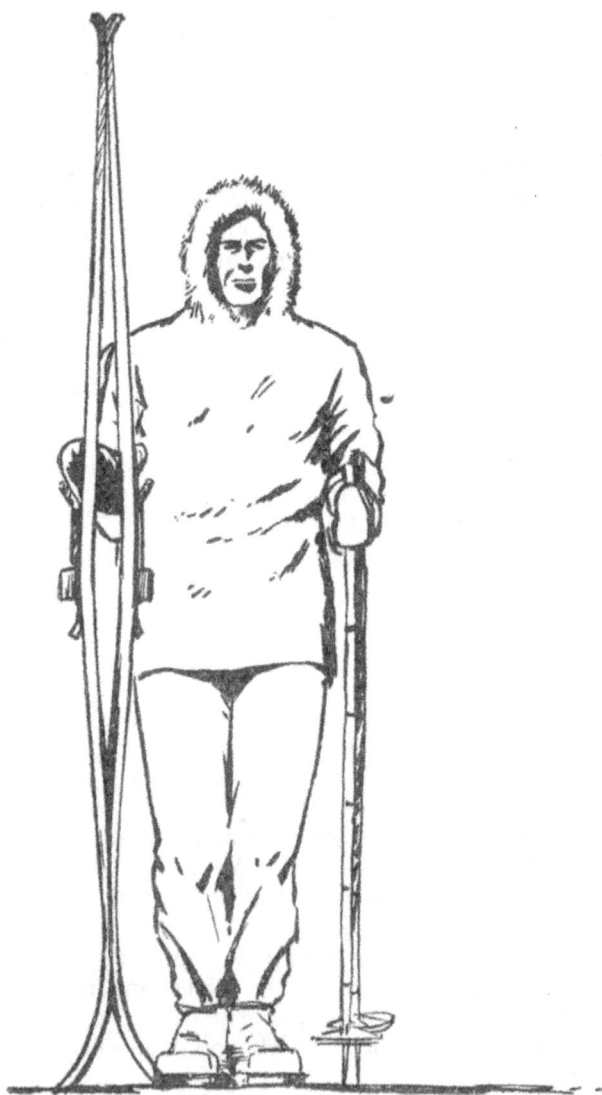

Figure 38. Position of order skis.

164

in FM 22–5, except that skis take place of rifle, and poles are held in the left hand.

(2) Skis being mounted: One ski must be kept in place.

d. FACINGS. (1) *To the flank* (fig. 39). The commands are: 1. RIGHT (LEFT) 2, FACE. At the command FACE, raise the right ski slightly and rotate it 45° to the right, using its heel as a pivot. (TWO) Move left ski alongside right ski. (THREE) Repeat first movement. (FOUR) Repeat second movement. Each pole is raised, moved, and placed with the corresponding ski.

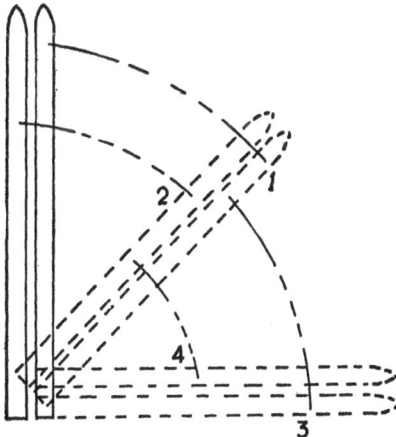

Figure 39. Movements for right face.

(2) *To the rear.* The commands are: 1. ABOUT, 2. FACE. At the command FACE, place the left pole alongside the left ski 18 inches in front of the toe iron and at the same time place the right pole alongside the right ski 18 inches behind the toe iron. (TWO) Raise the right leg until the ski is

perpendicular, its heel alongside the tip of the left ski. (THREE) Pivoting on the heel of the right ski, rotate and drop it until it is pointing in the opposite direction and place it by the right pole. (FOUR) Bring the left ski and pole around alongside the right ski in the new direction, placing the left pole by the toe iron of the left ski.

Note: This entire move is known as the kick turn. The poles are used throughout to maintain balance. On level ground the turn is to the right. On a mild slope the uphill ski leads; on a steep slope, the lower ski.

e. HAND SALUTE. The salute rendered is as prescribed in FM 22-5; the right hand is removed from the pole strap if time permits.

6. Steps and Marchings.

a. TAKING INTERVAL. No maneuver is made on skis without taking Ski Interval. The most convenient method of obtaining this is as follows: Being in line on mounted skis at normal interval. The commands are: 1. TO THE RIGHT (LEFT) FLANK, AT INTERVAL, 2. MARCH. At the command MARCH the right-flank man will step off straight to the front with the left ski. (TWO) Pivot the right ski 45° to the right and glide slightly. (THREE) Bring the left foot up parallel with the right, allowing it to glide slightly forward. (FOUR) Glide off at 45° again in the new direction. (FIVE) Bring the left ski parallel, skiing off in the new direction at a normal pace. As each preceding man starts his third step the following man starts his first step, and so on, the unit marching off in a column of files. When executing the command TO THE LEFT FLANK, AT INTERVAL, the left-flank man begins with the left ski, pivoting 45° and gliding on it. (TWO) Bring the right ski parallel and glide on it. (THREE, FOUR) Repeat the first two counts and start off in the new direction. At the conclusion of this movement the unit will be at ski interval, in column, but facing to the right or left.

b. STEPS. Movements begin on the left foot. Only quick time is used. Distance traveled with each step will vary with the snow.

c. BEING IN COLUMN, TO CHANGE DIRECTION. (1) The commands are: 1. COLUMN RIGHT (LEFT, HALF RIGHT, HALF LEFT), 2. MARCH. At the command MARCH the leading man takes a full step forward, then turns as in facing on skis, except that with each step a short slide is made. The fourth step is of full length in the new direction. Succeeding men follow in trace.

(2) *To march to the rear.* The commands are: 1. HALT, 2. ABOUT, 3. FACE, 4. FORWARD, 5. MARCH. At the command FACE, the inside ski is raised to the vertical position and rotated 180° in lowering until it reaches the position as described in paragraph 6*d* (2). The outside ski is then brought over the inside ski, and rotated 180° into position.

7. Manual of Skis.

a. POSITION OF ORDER SKIS. (See fig. 38.) Skis will be strapped together above the front cable throw, running surfaces together. Both skis will be held by the right hand at the rear of the foot plate, tips on line with and touching the toe of the right boot, edges facing forward. Poles, the ring of one placed over the shaft of the other, are held in the left hand, straps over the wrist, points 3 inches from and on line with the toe of the left boot.

b. BEING AT ORDER SKIS (fig. 40). The commands are: 1. RIGHT SHOULDER, 2. SKIS. At the command SKIS, lift the skis vertically until the upper arm is horizontal, at the same time grasping the skis with the left hand below the front cable throw. (TWO) Move the right hand down and grasp the skis just below the left hand. (THREE) Lower the skis so that the balance rests just back of the shoulder and skis are at an angle of 20° to the horizontal. (FOUR) Cut the left arm to the side.

Figure 40. Position of right shoulder skis.

c. BEING AT RIGHT SHOULDER SKIS. The commands are: 1. ORDER, 2. SKIS. At the command SKIS, grasp the skis with the left hand below the front cable throw. (TWO) Press down on the skis until they are in a vertical position about 18 inches from the ground. (THREE) Grasp the skis at the

168

rear of the toe irons with the right hand. (FOUR) Lower the skis gently to the ground and at the same time bring the left hand to the side.

d. BEING AT ORDER SKIS. The commands are: 1. INSPECTION, 2. SKIS. At the command SKIS, unstrap the skis, separate them, and place them so that the tip of each ski is on line with and three inches outside the toe of the corresponding boot and the running surfaces are turned to the front, one ski being held in each hand. The poles hang from the left wrist. After the inspecting officer has examined the edges, wax, etc., rotate the skis 180°. When the officer has passed, resume the position of attention.

e. BEING IN LINE, OPEN AND CLOSE RANKS. This movement is executed as prescribed in FM 22–5, except that each rank takes double the distance, that is, front rank, four steps; second rank, two steps; fourth rank, if any, four steps to the rear.

f. BEING IN LINE AT OPEN RANKS, TO MOUNT SKIS (fig. 41). The commands are: 1. MOUNT, 2. SKIS. At the command SKIS, move tips 2 feet to the front and at the same time take one step back with the right foot. (TWO) Lower skis gently to the ground. (THREE) Bring right foot forward and straddle skis. (FOUR) Place poles on ground parallel to skis and next to the left foot. (FIVE) Place feet in bindings as follows: unstrap skis; place running surfaces on ground six inches apart; hold toe strap with left hand, kick right boot into toe iron, and with both hands adjust heel spring around groove of boot; fasten cable throw so that boot is held firmly and fasten ankle straps by making a figure 8 loop around the ankle. Repeat procedure for left ski. Separate the poles and grasp both with the left hand. Insert right hand up through one strap so that the strap is around the back of the wrist. Grasp the pole with the right hand. Repeat with left hand and come to attention.

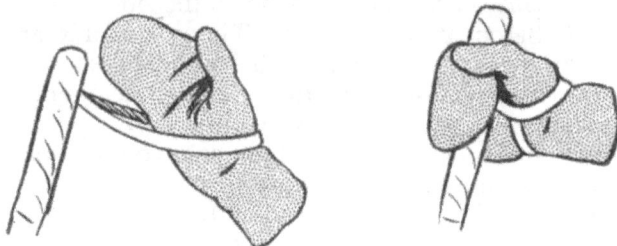

Figure 41. Proper use of pole straps.

g. To Dismount Skis. The commands are: 1. DISMOUNT, 2. SKIS. At the command skis, reverse the movements of MOUNT SKIS and assume position of ORDER SKIS.

h. At the command GROUND SKIS, execute the first two movements of MOUNT SKIS. (THREE) Come to attention.

i. Ski Salute. The movement is the same as in manual of arms for the rifle, except that the saluting hand need not be removed from the pole strap.

8. Squad and Platoon Drill.

a. To Stack Skis (fig. 42). (1) Being in line at open ranks and order skis, the commands are: 1. STACK, 2. SKIS. At the command skis, take 2 paces forward, lay skis down tips to the rear. (TWO) Separate the poles and place points in the ground about three feet apart, with the handle of the right pole crossed in front of the left, and make a **V** of the handles by interlacing each loop over with the opposite handle and crossing the handles. Grasp the poles with the left hand where they intersect. (THREE) Pick up skis with right hand and place in **V** formed by poles; at the same time tilt the poles

170

toward the ski tips for better balance. Assume the position of attention beside the bindings, with the stack to your right.

(2) At the commands, 1. TAKE, 2. SKIS, the movements of STACK SKIS are reversed and the position of ORDER SKIS is assumed.

b. To STACK EQUIPMENT (fig. 42). (1) Skis being stacked, the commands are: 1. STACK, 2. EQUIPMENT. At the command, EQUIPMENT, hang the rifle, pack and equipment over the extended heel of the skis, the rifle being slung on the right side.

(2) Equipment being stacked: at the commands 1. TAKE, 2. EQUIPMENT, the rifle, pack, and equipment are removed from the stack and the position of attention is resumed beside the stack.

(3) In ski drill, the rifle, when carried, is always slung.

Section III. ELEMENTARY SKIING

9. Falling.

a. Falling causes fatigue, injury, and loss of time. It is imperative, therefore, that the soldier eventually learn to ski without falling often. The soldier should also learn how to fall so as to avoid injury.

b. The following precautions are suggested to prevent falls:

(1) Resist the fall and recover your equilibrium wherever possible.

(2) Concentrate on riding out the imminent fall.

(3) Drop into a deeper crouch.

(4) If falling backward, reach forward with the arms, at the same time moving one foot back underneath the body; reverse the procedure if you are falling forward.

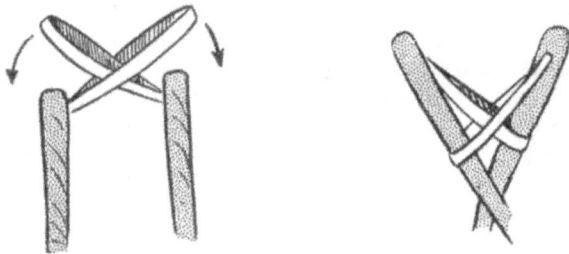

① MAKING V OF POLES.

② COMPLETED STACK.

Figure 42. Stacking skis and equipment.

(5) If falling to the side, lift the ski on that side by a slight jump upward and place it in its proper place underneath you.

(6) If the skis are widely separated and a fall between them seems inevitable, push strongly with one foot so as to force all the weight over onto the

other ski, then lift the first one and place it in proper running position.

c. When a fall is imminent, the following precautions will usually prevent injury:

(1) Land on one hip, and, if the arms are extended, the body and skis will slide to a stop as a unit. It is almost impossible to be injured in falling in this manner.

(2) In a sideward fall, try to keep the body from rolling along the snow. This is best done by extending the arms sideward and stretching the body out at full length away from the skis. The body is kept straight, for if the knees are bent and the skier lands on the snow on one knee, it will be twisted backward, and it or the ankle may be injured.

(3) In a fall forward at any speed, it is best to duck the head and roll onto the back.

(4) While falling, the skis should be pulled free of the snow, brought parallel, and as close together as possible. This effort should be made in even the most violent of cartwheels.

(5) When footing is lost on a steep slope keep the skis below the body and as close to the slope as possible; then the running position on the traverse can sometimes be regained if the skier moves his weight forward and outward.

d. (1) After a fall, especially if the skis have become entangled, the skier should think of what to do before attempting to rise. Beginners often try to get to their feet with the skis pointing downhill, whereupon the skis run out from under them and they fall again. A little planning before attempting to rise may prevent an injury.

(2) After a severe fall, the skis can usually be untangled if the skier rolls onto his back, lifts his skis in the air, and realigns them from that position. If the skis are on the uphill side, he should

roll onto his back and bring them downhill before attempting to get up. When the skis are below the skier, across the slope, and tucked up under the body, it is simple to push with the poles on the uphill side, roll onto the feet, and stand up. Snow should be brushed from the clothing before it melts and dampens the cloth.

10. Walking on the Level.

a. This is the simplest movement in skiing. The arms and legs move as in marching on the level, except that the feet and skis are not lifted off the snow, but slide forward in a gliding motion. If the weight of the skis is lifted by the leg muscles every time a step is taken, the many thousands of steps taken during the day's march will result in early fatigue. Let the snow carry the weight of the ski.

b. The tops of the poles should be ahead of the rings when the propelling push is made. Keep the elbows close to the sides and the rings of the poles close to the skis. Thrust with the arm and shoulder muscles as in rising from an easy chair. Don't hold the poles upright like a staff, or place them far out like an outrigger. Use the poles to push ahead, and to prevent sliding back when climbing. Instead of merely placing one foot in front of the other alternately as in ordinary walking, the skier thrusts his foot and the ski forward with the full weight of the body upon them in a long stride, and, at the same time, accompanies it by a push on the opposite pole. The result will be a gliding motion that gives added distance to each step. It is this slide at the end of each stride that makes skis the most efficient means of foot travel over snow-covered terrain.

11. Sidestep.

The sidestep is the simplest, but one of the least

efficient, methods of climbing a slope. Standing with skis across the slope, force the uphill edge of the skis into the snow to prevent slipping down the hill sideways. Move the uphill ski two or so feet up the slope, then bring the lower one up beside it. This action is repeated until the slope has been climbed. If the skis are not placed squarely across the slope they may start to run forward or backward. Such a method of climbing lifts the skier up the slope by the muscles of one leg only. Consequently, the sidestep is useful only on short climbs where more efficient climbing methods cannot be used. To avoid floundering on steep slopes covered with deep, soft snow, leave as much space as possible between each pair of steps. This space usually provides enough support for the snow to keep both it and the skier on the slope.

12. Traverse.

The traverse is the least tiring method of walking up a slope. With the skis edged as in the sidestep, the skier walks as though skiing on the level, choosing an easy angle of ascent. He does not walk directly up the slope but zig-zags up it with kick turns at each switchback. The distance traveled on any one traverse will depend on the terrain and the objective at the top of the slope. Normally, the longer each traverse is, the better. Kick turns dissipate energy.

13. Sidestep Traverse.

a. A variation of the traverse that permits a faster climb is the sidestep traverse. By raising each ski slightly as he brings it forward the skier can set it uphill a few inches, making a slight gain in elevation with each step.

175

b. When this maneuver is used in deep soft snow, each step will require packing the snow for the full length of each ski. It should, therefore, be abandoned and the simple traverse used, where only one-third as much snow is packed with each step. Point the poles backward, and push on them with the hands to help prevent the skis from slipping backward. It is often helpful to push on the top of the downhill pole instead of on the strap.

14. Herringbone.

(Figure 43.) A more rapid—and more tiring— method of climbing is the herringbone. Face uphill, spread the skis apart in a wide V, tips apart. To prevent the skis from slipping back, edge them sharply by dropping the knees forward and slightly together, and push on the tops of the poles. Move the arms and legs exactly as in walking. When the left foot is moving forward, the push on the left pole helps to keep the sharply edged right ski from sliding backward. As the left ski is being set into the snow, the right pole is planted firmly just below the right foot, so that a push on it will help keep the left ski from sliding backward as the right ski moves forward. Chief fault of the herringbone is its inefficiency. The position, being unnatural, calls for an unusual use of muscles; skis must be lifted too far; a track must be packed for the entire length of the ski with each step in soft snow; traction is often uncertain. A deliberate herringbone, executed with rhythm, is nevertheless very useful in climbing short pitches.

15. Herringbone Turn.

For changing direction of the traverse of moderate slopes the herringbone turn is often most efficient.

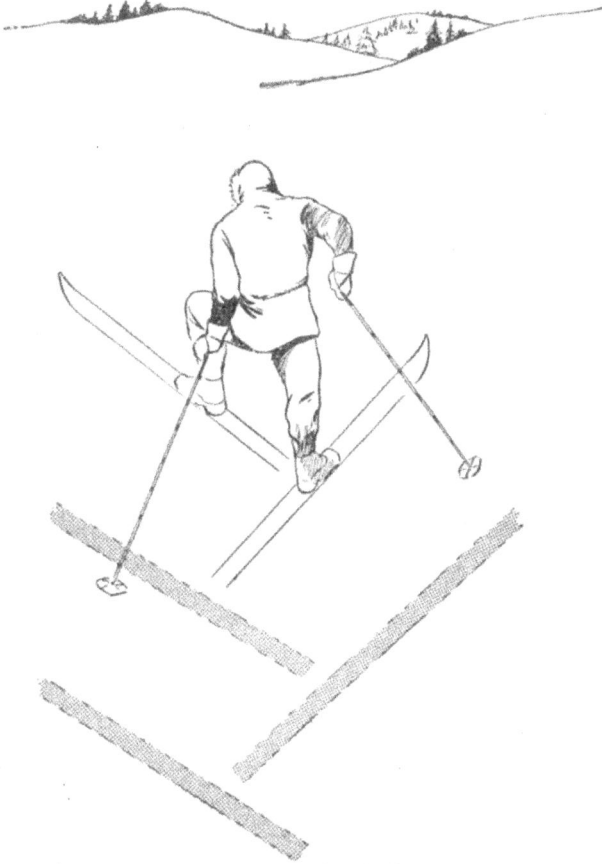

Figure 43. The herringbone.

for it is not necessary to stop momentarily as in the
kick turn. From a traverse, start the herringbone
by turning the upper ski about 45° uphill and
thrust it firmly into the snow on its upper edge.
Turn the lower ski uphill about 20°. With the next

step, turn the inside ski another 45°, place it firmly on its inside edge, and bring the outside ski up into herringbone position. Thence continue around the turn. On the final step with the outside ski, swing its heel up until the ski is across the slope, and kick it firmly into the snow on its upper edge and start off in the new direction of traverse. Considerable reliance must be placed on the ski poles and proper edging of the skis for support while making the turn.

16. Kick Turn.

See ABOUT FACE, paragraph 5*d*.

17. Straight Downhill Run.

Skiing downhill is neither difficult nor complex. The novice should first learn how to slide downhill on smooth, easy snow, then over bumps and through difficult snow. The weight should be evenly distributed on both skis, for this is the most natural way to maintain balance, and is the most stable. The position of the body with respect to the skis is important. (See fig. 44.) In the correct downhill running position, the *ankles are bent forward*, as well as the knees; the upper body is in a slight crouch, and, at the same time, leans slightly forward, so that the skier is working with gravity instead of against it. If he fails to lean forward his skis will travel faster than his body and will cause him to fall backwards. The hands, arms, and ski poles are held away from the side to produce the same stabilizing effect that a tightrope walker gains when extending his hands and arms sideward. When the snow is smooth and balance easy to maintain, hands and poles should be closer to the sides than when running fast or over difficult snow. In variable snow, in which the speed of the skis is likely to change suddenly, modify the straight downhill–run position as shown in figure 45. One foot should be slightly ahead of the other; one pole should be ahead of normal position, the other to the rear. This position enables skier to maintain equilibrium when speed varies suddenly because of changing snow texture. This will increase the forward-backward stability.

Figure 44. Position for straight, downhill run.

18. Traversing Downhill.

The beginner who has learned to choose and run a gradual route of descent across a slope can, by traversing and kick-turning, travel over a great variety of terrain. The greater part of the weight should be placed on the lower ski and the upper ski advanced a few inches. To keep from slipping downhill, the skis may be edged well into the slope, and are controlled more with the knees than with

179

the ankles. At the same time, the upper body should lean away from the slope to preserve the balance. To keep the tips from drifting downhill, the downhill shoulder is lower than the upper, and is moved slightly forward (fig. 45).

Figure 45. Downhill traversing position.

Section IV. ELEMENTARY CROSS COUNTRY TECHNIQUE

19. Waxes.

The running surface of the ski is kept from direct contact with the snow by layers of a composite substance called, in general, wax. The use of wax serves the following purposes:

a. Prevents absorption of moisture by the wood of the running surface.

b. Makes the skis slide easily.

c. Prevents the skis from sliding backward during climbs.

20. Types and Uses.

a. BASE WAX. (1) Base wax is used to protect the wood of the running surface from moisture. It is intended to be durable, to stick tightly to the wood, to hold well the additional waxes later applied, and to slide well if these are worn off.

(2) Before a base wax is applied, the surface should be clean and dry. It should be free from old wax to permit the base to penetrate and hold well to the wood. To clean the surface, first scrape well with a sharp-edged instrument, then wipe with a cloth soaked in some non–oily solvent such as gasoline, or cleaning or lighter fluid, and finally rub with fine sandpaper. When the base becomes worn in spots, it may be touched up temporarily, and a full coat of wax applied later.

b. RUNNING AND CLIMBING WAX. (1) Additional waxes are used either to make the skis slide easily or to prevent them from sliding backward in climbs, or for both purposes simultaneously. Choice of wax depends on the route and the condition of the snow. For instructions in the use of ski waxes under varying conditions, see TM 10–275. If the skis will not hold with a thin layer of a given wax, the skier adds more of the same wax and stamps the foot slightly with each step. This will enable him to climb moderately steep slopes more readily. Upon reaching the top, he smooths the running surfaces by moving the skis back and forth in their packed tracks. This motion and the first few feet of the down-hill run will usually break loose any accumulation of snow crystals caught in the thicker wax layer. Sometimes a thick layer of the same wax, or a layer of a softer wax, on the running surface below the binding and foot plate, will enable the skier to obtain good climbing and running qualities on the same application. Also, the same effect is gained if the wax surface is left rough, as it is applied, or if diagonal marks—"jeep-tread" pattern —are made on the ski with the wax that is added.

(2) The skier should never attempt to make his skis run slowly by waxing with a softer wax. The skis will then run jerkily, and cause unsteadiness and insecurity. The skis should be waxed to slide properly, and excess speed should be controlled by turns and sideslips. Excess speed cannot be checked satisfactorily by the use of a climbing wax. A fast ski is a controllable ski.

21. Climbers.

a. If climbers are not available, they can be improvised by winding small rope around the ski in several wraps from binding to heel—or, if the rope is long enough, from tip to heel—and tying it in several places underneath. With climbers the skier can ascend a steeper gradient than with wax, and he will be able to climb in all snow conditions as well. In addition, by waxing the skis with hard wax, he can be assured that they will slide well when the climbers are removed.

b. Over undulating terrain the skier will lose too much time if he puts on or takes off climbers more than once an hour; it is better to wax properly for climbing and running. Climbers should be used only when climbing long slopes (1,000 or more vertical ft.).

22. Two Step.

a. This step (fig. 46) permits attaining more speed on the level and on a downhill slope than can be obtained by the one step. It also provides a means of resting the muscles by using them differently. For purposes of instruction, the skier starts without using the poles and proceeds as follows:

(1) He places the skis together and bends knees slightly.

(2) He straightens the body and takes a short step with the left foot.

(3) He lunges into a long glide on the right foot, placing all his weight on it.

(4) The left ski heel may be raised from the snow at the start of the lunge. The glide should be as long and smooth as possible. While gliding, he brings the left foot slowly ahead, preparatory to repeating the two steps, which should be started before the momentum of the glide is lost.

b. After the step and lunge is mastered, he learns to use the poles smoothly and efficiently for added power. As he takes the first step, he starts both poles and arms forward. When he lunges, he places the poles even with and close to the ski tip and smoothly powers the lunge by bending the body well forward, first pulling on the poles, then, as his body reaches them, pushing on them, bending the knees to increase the power of the thrust.

c. The cycle is in the two-count rhythm of step, lunge, and thrust; step, lunge, and thrust. The glide is always on the same foot. An extra short step may be taken occasionally to change the glide to the other ski, and to employ a new set of muscles. If

183

the two step is to be used for long periods, it must be deliberate and rhythmic, slow enough to let the skier relax during the glide. A two step taken as he enters a dip will speed him through and help him up the other side—a maneuver that can be used frequently.

Figure 46. Two step.

23. Three Step.

When going is easier, or as an alternate to the two step, the three step may be used. The skier moves in about the same fashion as in the two step but inserts one more step. This brings the alternate foot forward on each glide. As a consequence different muscles are called into use and the step is less tiring.

Section V. TURNS

24. Snow Plow and Snow Plow Turn.

a. GENERAL. The usual question of every beginner as he begins his first downhill run on skis is, "How can I slow down?" perhaps, if an obstacle gets in his way, he will be more interested in asking, "How can I miss it?" The answer to both questions lies in a simple position of skis and body known as the snow plow. It is also a fundamental part of other turns to be described.

b. SNOW PLOW (fig. 47). (1) From a straight running position, the skis are moved so that they resemble a **V** plow; the tips are held almost touching one another; the tails are pushed far apart—as

Figure 47. Snowplow position.

185

far as will permit the skier to feel at ease and capable of moving. His heels are in contact with the skis at all times. The knees are pressed inward and forward to a position even with the toes. The upper part of the body is held almost erect, the hips well forward.

(2) The skier must get the "feel" of how much the skis are riding on their edges. The most common fault is too much edging. This causes many types of difficulties, the most frequent one being crossing of the skis. If, when moving forward, either edge bites into the snow, the edged ski will keep its direction and cross the other. Free play of both knees and ankles is essential to control of the edges.

(3) To change from the normal straight running position to the snow plow position, the heels are pushed out gradually; more and more weight is put on them as the skis slow down. In a simple snow plow position, the weight is equally distributed between the feet; the position of the body is one of symmetry. The wider the V of the skis, the more friction there is with the snow and the less will be the speed. Use of the edges to obtain the same effect should be rather limited. The skis should slide forward almost as if they were caressing the snow.

(4) Use of the snow plow for stopping is very limited. On steep slopes and with great speed it is practically impossible to stop with it. It should be well studied and practiced, however, for in various turns the ability to snow plow properly is indispensable. Although the snow plow is a tiring position to hold for long, it sometimes must be used; for example, in a descent which is too dangerous to take straight, yet is too narrow to turn in.

(5) So long as the weight is equal on both skis,

and the body is in a symmetrical position, the skis will move in a straight line downhill. Speed can be regulated and controlled by opening the **V** as the slope gets steeper, or by reducing it as the slope becomes more gentle. The knees are kept well forward, but not together. The skier bends forward at the ankles, not at the waist.

c. SNOW PLOW TURN. (1) When the skier is running in the snow plow position and shifts his weight onto one ski and pushes the shoulder on that side forward, he will begin to turn to the other side in a snow plow turn, because the ski with the most weight on it will have the most friction with the snow and will tend to run in that direction. If he wishes to turn left, the ski pointing that way is weighted—in this case, the right ski. To turn the other way, the weight is placed on the left ski. The first action in shifting the weight is made by the knee that is going to carry the weight. It is pressed smoothly forward until it is over the toe of the foot, at the same time keeping the heel flat on the ski. When this knee is bent, the weight is automatically pushed over onto it by the other leg, because there is no change in the amount of bend in the other knee. The weighted knee is pushed forward by the shoulder and hip, which is pivoted to the front, over the weighted ski. As the skis come around in the turn, they should be held in the snow plow position throughout, with the points always as close together as possible. The proper amount of edging can be controlled only if the knees are pressed well forward. To make a smooth and rounded turn, the inside ski has to be held flat on the snow; otherwise, it will not follow through the turn. An edged ski has too much resistance to the snow, and may prevent completion of the turn, or catch so that the other ski will run away from it. The final position of one turn is the starting position of the next.

(2) From the very beginning the skier should try to get a certain amount of rhythm and curve to the turns instead of jerking them. The weight should not be thrown suddenly on the outside ski, but shifted gradually, at the same time pivoting with the hips and shoulders. If the snow is difficult or deep, every attempt is made to keep the skis flat during the turn. Allow the skis to slide *through* the snow, rather than trying to make them slide on top of the snow by edging. A help in turning in such snow is to push the outside shoulder forward as the weight is brought onto the outside foot.

25. The Stem Turn.

a. The stem turn (fig. 48), in principle, is nothing but a snow plow turn, except that the snow plow position is not held from one turn to the next. Between turns the skis are brought together and parallel in a traverse across the slope. In the traverse, the two most common faults are leaning in toward the slope and letting the upper ski lag behind the lower ski. Either fault results in an unbalanced position.

b. The speed on the traverse is usually greater than can be managed in the stem turn. Learn to reduce your speed so that you can enter the turn with confidence and security. The motion that accomplishes this is the counterstem. It is so important a part of ski technique that it is used in all types of modern turns, even, to a slight extent, in those at highest speed. To counterstem, the heel of the lower ski is moved downhill to form a small snow plow, and, at the same time, the uphill shoulder is moved backward to force more of the weight onto the lower, or inside, ski thus checking the speed. The motions should be done carefully and smoothly. To allow the inside ski to be moved into a **V**, the weight should be shifted onto the upper ski momentarily, and then shifted *smoothly* back onto the lower ski as it is moved outward and downward. The motion is done with very little

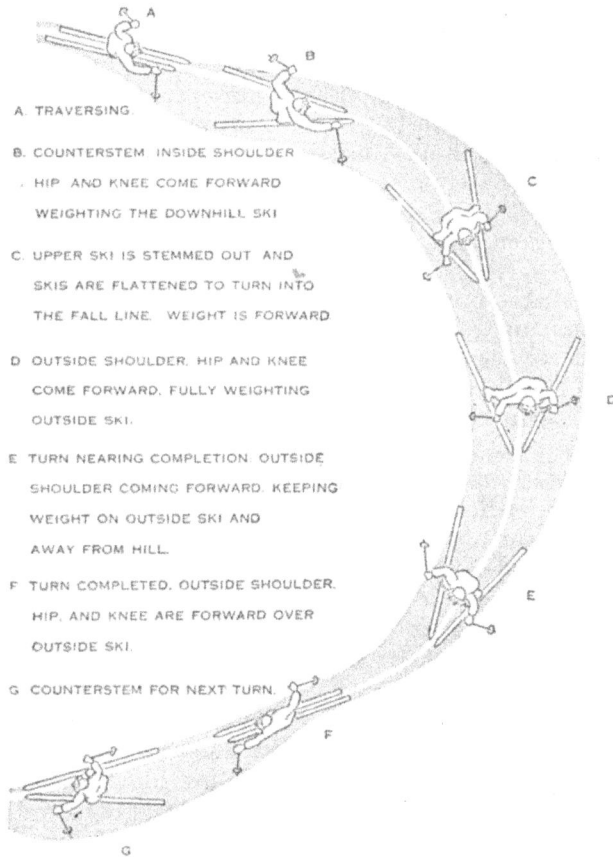

A. TRAVERSING.

B. COUNTERSTEM. INSIDE SHOULDER.
   HIP AND KNEE COME FORWARD
   WEIGHTING THE DOWNHILL SKI.

C. UPPER SKI IS STEMMED OUT AND
   SKIS ARE FLATTENED TO TURN INTO
   THE FALL LINE. WEIGHT IS FORWARD.

D. OUTSIDE SHOULDER, HIP AND KNEE
   COME FORWARD, FULLY WEIGHTING
   OUTSIDE SKI.

E. TURN NEARING COMPLETION. OUTSIDE
   SHOULDER COMING FORWARD. KEEPING
   WEIGHT ON OUTSIDE SKI AND
   AWAY FROM HILL.

F. TURN COMPLETED. OUTSIDE SHOULDER,
   HIP, AND KNEE ARE FORWARD OVER
   OUTSIDE SKI.

G. COUNTERSTEM FOR NEXT TURN.

Figure 48. Stem turn.

189

edging of the lower ski. The outward and forward motion of the knee will be enough to give proper control. To the beginner and average skier the counterstem is not so much a means of checking speed as of bringing the whole body into action. For every rhythmical swinging movement needs a counterswing; it is the source of all the "body swing." In bad snow and at low speed it is not necessary actually to stem the lower ski when weight is transferred to it. The transfer of weight to the inside ski is still important, however, for only by this transfer can the outside ski be stemmed out. In ordinary snow at usual speeds the inside ski will be counterstemmed.

    c. When the speed has been checked enough to permit entrance into the turn, the skier presses the knees farther forward and the heel of the upper ski slowly outward in a wide snow plow. At the same time the skis are flattened against the snow, and the weight is forward. The front part of the skis will then start drifting down the hill and begin the turn. The weight of the body is gradually shifted toward the outside ski. By the time the skis are pointing downhill—or are on the fall line—the weight will be about even on the skis; but after this point all the weight will be transferred onto the outside ski. To aid in moving the weight, the outside shoulder and hip are pivoted smoothly and slowly around from the back position they were in during the counterstem into a forward position at the end of the turn. The weight must be on the outside ski or the turn will not be made. When halfway through the turn the skier will be, for a short moment, in a symmetrical snow plow position heading directly down the slope. At first he will want to lean uphill and onto the inside ski; but if he does, the turn will stop and he will accelerate down the slope until he falls backward. However, if he leans more forward and onto the outside ski, the turn will swing around smoothly and under perfect control. Both knees must be bent well forward, especially the outside knee that bears most of the weight. The inside ski is kept ahead of the outer one and well flattened against the snow. He must have the inside of the ski flat on the snow during the last half of the turn to keep it from catching and pulling to the rear. The last phase of the turn should be done in a relaxed manner. The inside ski will join the other of its own accord only if the turn is completed and all the weight placed on the lower ski. The proper stem turn will carve a smooth semicircular track of even radius. The steeper the slope, the wider must be the snow plow during the turn, and the more important it is that the skier complete the turn and start back across, rather than down, the slope. The turn should be held until the skier is ready to traverse. It is important to begin the turn correctly, for then there is a very good chance of finishing it well, even if a small mistake is made during the turn. On the contrary, if the turn is started incorrectly, the skier will probably end up in difficulty.

d. It is difficult to make the stem turn without using the counterstem; all the speed of the traverse will have to be checked by stemming with the uphill ski, which has little body weight on it, offers little resistance to the snow, and hence cannot easily reduce the speed. If an attempt is made to put weight on it to increase the friction, the skis immediately begin to turn whether the skier is ready or not. Most of the time the snow plow will be too narrow, and the speed will be too great, causing the turns to run out of control. Much more strength will be required. The turn will often "run away" unless a gradual, and hence slower, route of traverse is chosen.

   e. In soft snow the skis are kept flatter than on hard snow, so they will slide through the snow sideways. If edged, they tend to wedge against the snow and either will not move sideways at all or will require too much energy to push the mass of snow around. A firm swing without shoulders and hips will help the skier to turn easily in deeper snow.

   f. On breakable crust take great care not to shift the weight fully onto one ski or it will break through and trip you. Wait at least until the outside ski points straight down the slope. If the shift is made too early and the ski breaks through, the turn cannot be made. If the ski breaks through after it points downhill, the skier's weight will be above it and will probably force the turn around.

   g. The stem turn demands much practice, in every kind of snow, on easy and steep slopes. Even the best skier will come back to the stem turn in bad and difficult snow, for it provides the best control of any turn; by its use a soldier can travel in any snow on any skiable slope.

26. Side Slipping.

Before the skier can perform the advanced turns well, he must learn to sideslip properly and easily, for the basic principle of a ski turn is most easily studied and learned in the sideslip (fig. 49). The skis are placed across the slope a few inches apart, the upper ski slightly ahead of the lower and the skis edged into the hill; the legs are bent forward at the ankles and the body held in a relaxed posi tion. The sideslip is started by moving the knees forward and downhill. This flattens the edges of the skis against the snow and permits them to slide down the slope sideways. To prevent their moving out from under the body, the skier leans slightly downhill at the time the skis are flattened. To control the speed of sideslip, the knees are pressed forward and slightly uphill. If either the tips or the heels of the skis tend to slide faster, he counteracts this by leaning toward the opposite end of the ski. By this same shifting of the weight he can change a simple sideslip into a downward skidding traverse, either forward or backward. The sideslip can be used on very steep slopes and in soft snow. It is the

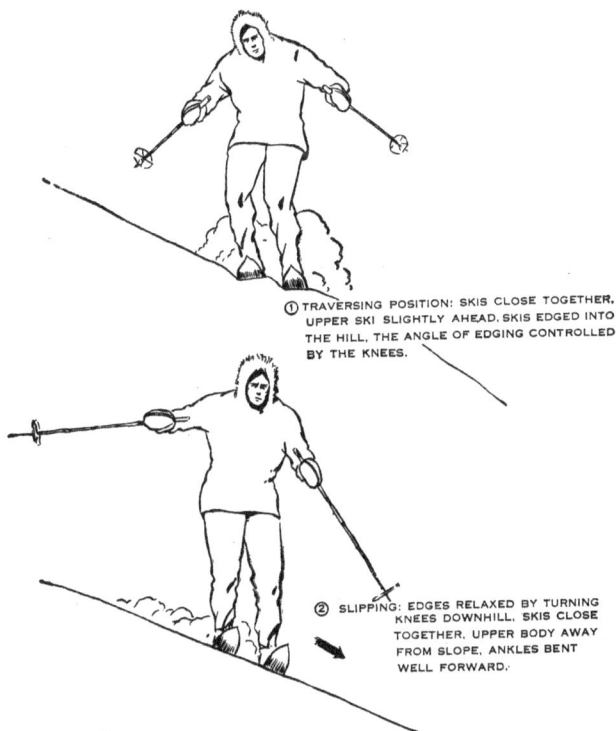

① TRAVERSING POSITION: SKIS CLOSE TOGETHER, UPPER SKI SLIGHTLY AHEAD. SKIS EDGED INTO THE HILL, THE ANGLE OF EDGING CONTROLLED BY THE KNEES.

② SLIPPING: EDGES RELAXED BY TURNING KNEES DOWNHILL, SKIS CLOSE TOGETHER, UPPER BODY AWAY FROM SLOPE, ANKLES BENT WELL FORWARD.

Figure 49. Sideslipping.

193

best method of losing altitude rapidly on skis without gaining much speed.

27. Uphill Christiania.

a. The uphill christiania is used mainly to stop the skier when he is traversing. During a downhill traverse, he must first pull the lower shoulder back, then move it forward while the weight is moved onto the lower ski. Skis must not be edged into the slope nearly as much as in the traverse, or they will not slide sideways. The heels of the skis will, when the edges are properly relaxed, drop downhill, causing a sliding turn uphill, which will stop the skier faster than a simple skid sideways.

b. In preparation for later turns, the skier should practice the uphill christiania on progressively steeper traverses until he is able to turn into the hill from a direct descent.

28. Advanced Stem Turn.

This turn aids the transition from stem turn to stem christiania, and is taught on a steeper slope than is used for stem–turn instruction. The skier starts the turn as he would start the stem; however, he need not spread the heels so far, for on the steeper slope the skis will turn downhill as soon as he presses his knees and weight forward and toward the fall line. After the turn has started, he slowly moves the outside shoulder, hip, and knee forward and pushes out the heel of the outside ski. When he has reached the fall line, he pivots forward swiftly but smoothly with the outside shoulder, hip, and knee, thus returning to the position of the next traverse by bringing the skis together and skidding, as in a christiania into the hill.

29. Stem Christiania.

a. The stem christiania (fig. 50) is the most advanced turn to be learned by the soldier. It is a good turn in both soft snow and hard snow, on steep or gradual slopes, and can be used at moderate speed or high speed.

b. To start the turn more speed is necessary than with the stem turn. The counterstem is made with

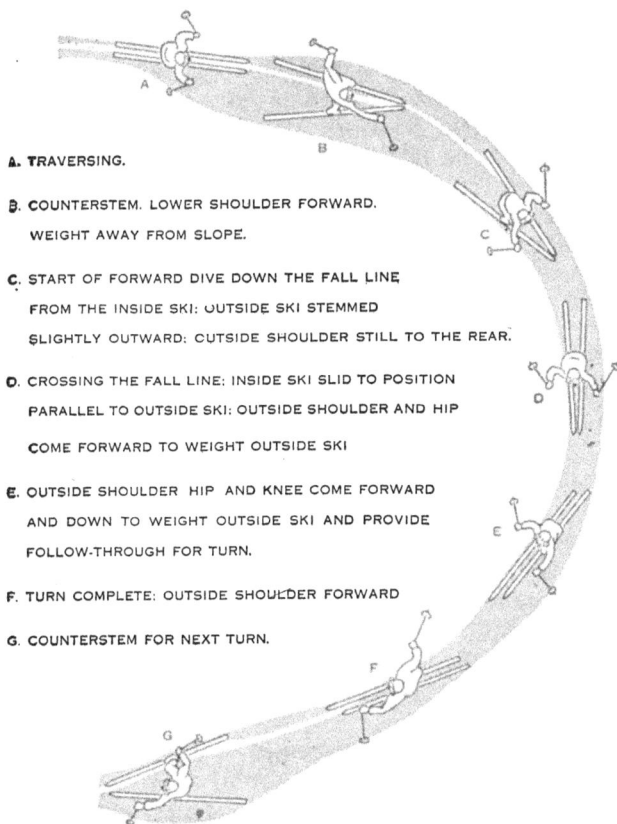

A. TRAVERSING.

B. COUNTERSTEM. LOWER SHOULDER FORWARD. WEIGHT AWAY FROM SLOPE.

C. START OF FORWARD DIVE DOWN THE FALL LINE FROM THE INSIDE SKI: OUTSIDE SKI STEMMED SLIGHTLY OUTWARD: OUTSIDE SHOULDER STILL TO THE REAR.

D. CROSSING THE FALL LINE: INSIDE SKI SLID TO POSITION PARALLEL TO OUTSIDE SKI: OUTSIDE SHOULDER AND HIP COME FORWARD TO WEIGHT OUTSIDE SKI

E. OUTSIDE SHOULDER HIP AND KNEE COME FORWARD AND DOWN TO WEIGHT OUTSIDE SKI AND PROVIDE FOLLOW-THROUGH FOR TURN.

F. TURN COMPLETE: OUTSIDE SHOULDER FORWARD

G. COUNTERSTEM FOR NEXT TURN.

Figure 50. Stem christiania.

195

the lower ski, but is even narrower than in the advanced stem because it is not used to check speed. The shoulder, hip, and knee will come down and forward to weight the lower ski. From this point the outside ski is stemmed slightly and both skis are so flattened that they will run naturally into the fall line with the forward lean of the body. This forward lean is gained by rising forward from the inside or lower knee and diving down the fall line with the skis still in a slight stem. Now the outside shoulder, hip, and knee play an important part. So far they have come only slightly forward from their rear position. But as the skis are floating free down the fall line, the outside shoulder, hip, and knee come forward, throwing the weight onto the outside ski. The outside shoulder must follow through and forward until the very end of the turn, but must not twist so far that it crosses the body and throws the weight into the hill.

c. There is a slight down-up-down motion in this turn that is not noticed in the others. The body goes down first to weight the lower counter-stemmed ski and then must come up and forward to throw the weight onto the outside ski. This upward movement at the fall line helps unweight the skis, allowing them to turn easily; as the weight comes down on the outside ski, it holds the turn.

d. It is important not to hurry the turn; make it, instead, in "slow motion." Many turns end poorly because the skid is started too soon, and the turn is finished before the new traverse is reached. Let your linked stem christianias be S-turns, not Z's.

30. Lifted Stem Christiania.

One of the best and most useful turns for soft or heavy snow and a heavy pack is the short-radius lifted stem christiania. It is done at a speed about as low as that of the stem turn. The counterstem is done as in the stem turn, except that it may at times consist merely of transferring all weight forward onto the lower ski. At the point of full development of the counterstem the lower pole is placed firmly in the snow at a point below and ahead of the inside ski tip. The outside ski is pushed out into a wide stem before the weight is shifted onto it and the fall line reached. A vigorous swing forward of the upper shoulder and body, combined with a strong push off the inside ski, forces the outside ski around in a short-radius circle. The outside ski must be stemmed out far enough so that it points in the new direction before the actual turning starts. Then when the weight is shifted the turn is practically completed. The outward swing of the heel of the outside ski is further increased by a powerful push on the inside pole as the ski passes through the fall line and comes below the point of the pole. The inside ski will not slide around on such a short circle, so it must be picked up and placed alongside the other ski. Although the turn can be done without the use of the pole, the soldier will make full use of the poles so that maximum stability and safety will be maintained. The combined thrust from the inside ski and the inside pole will serve to drive the outside ski around through the heaviest snow. The turn is more useful than any other for running when snow is poor and turns must be short and accurate.

Section VI. ADVANCED CROSS-COUNTRY TECHNIQUE

31. General.

The soldier who has learned his fundamentals must learn to ski with a pack and rifle before putting the fundamentals into practice in cross-country marches. In addition, he must learn certain new movements which will be of the greatest value when he is skiing with a heavy pack over difficult terrain.

32. Skiing with Pack and Rifle.

a. All the basic movements must be mastered, first with a light pack, and later, the load should be gradually increased to rifle and full pack.

b. In the downhill running position in soft and variable snow the skis will be held about 4 inches apart, one ski about a foot ahead of the other. On hard snow the skis will be about 9 inches apart to improve balance and stability.

c. When turning with a pack, the skier will probably use the stem turn more often than the stem christiania. Emphasis must be laid on a smooth and powerful knee and shoulder movement.

d. Climbers will always be used for uphill work of any great distance.

e. Skiing with a pack and rifle on steep slopes, narrow paths, soft snow, hard snow, breakable crust, etc., will present difficulties for which the ski soldier must be prepared by practice with the various skiing turns and movements described in the preceding paragraphs. In addition, the following items of technique will be found useful.

33. Running in Variable Snow.

The skier must watch and judge carefully the snow conditions in the path ahead so that he can maneuver to offset sudden changes in speed caused by changing snow texture. When skiing from soft into hard snow, he increases his forward lean, since the skis will run faster on hard snow and will otherwise run out from under him. Conversely, when running from hard into soft snow, he moves his weight back just before he comes into the slower snow, in which the skis will tend to hang back. When changes in snow texture come so close together that the body position cannot be changed rapidly enough, one ski should be placed a foot or two ahead of the other one, and, at the same time, the body is dropped into a deep crouch. The lower the center of gravity of the body, the greater the stability. Lateral balance can be increased by extending the arms sideways in the manner used naturally when one tries to walk a straight line. The same technique can be used for running through sharp dips or deep drifts. The Telemark position—one ski about 1½ feet to the front, the other about the same distance to the rear—should be assumed thus increasing forward-backward stability.

34. Running on Icy Snow or Crust.

Stability is improved by running in a slight snowplow position. Skis will chatter in a turn if they are edged too much, but if the skier's weight is well forward and he carefully controls the edges, he can turn as smoothly on icy snow or crust as on a softer surface. More space should be allowed between men, inasmuch as turns cannot be as accurately placed as on softer snow. When running down a trail covered with icy ruts, the skier should not attempt to slow down by using a snowplow. Instead, he should sideslip with both skis. The snowplow is dangerous because the tips may catch in a rut and throw him forward. It is well, when skiing on icy snow or crust, to be adequately protected by clothing, including mittens on the hands. Otherwise, falls may result in cuts and abrasions.

35. Running on Variable Terrain.

When the slope steepens, the skis slide faster, so the skier must increase his forward lean when he begins to descend a sudden, steep pitch. Similarly, when the slope flattens out, the weight must be moved back slightly. When riding over bumpy snow, stability is greatly increased by allowing the knees and skis to move up and down to conform to the changes in the surface of the snow in the manner of shock absorbers (fig. 51). The body should ride on as even a line as possible; skis are brought up toward the chest as they approach a bump, and

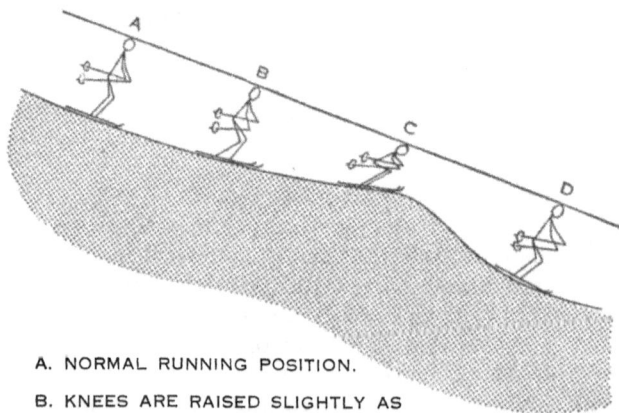

A. NORMAL RUNNING POSITION.

B. KNEES ARE RAISED SLIGHTLY AS
   BUMP IS APPROACHED

C. KNEES ARE FULLY RAISED TO A POSITION
   THAT WILL PERMIT THE HEAD AND BODY
   TO RIDE IN A STRAIGHT LINE DOWN THE SLOPE.

D. KNEES ARE PUSHED DOWN AGAIN TO
   NORMAL RUNNING POSITION.

Figure 51. Riding bumps.

are pushed down as the hollows pass under the skis. If a bump is too large to be taken with knee action alone, the soldier will probably go into the air on the other side. To increase stability when landing, he should land with one ski well ahead of the other.

36. Step Turn.

The step turn is useful for making turns in breakable crust, or other difficult snow, on gentle slopes where the speed is not too great. It is done by completely weighting the outside ski and at the same time turning the body slightly to the inside. Raise the tip of the inside ski and move it a foot or so to the inside. Place the weight on that ski, and at the same time raising the tip of the outside ski and bringing it alongside the inner ski. This cycle is repeated, each series of two steps moving the skier in a new direction. Care should be taken to lift the tip of each ski out of the snow before the heel comes out; this prevents the ski from catching in the snow and causing a fall. When making the step turn, the skier should lean inside a little, bend the knees, and not try to start the turn with the outside ski.

37. Skating Stride.

a. The skating stride (fig. 52) is a pleasant variation of the normal walking steps for use on gradual descents in hard snow with a thin soft surface. It is very useful for rapid and accurate changes of direction in wood running.

b. The movement of skis and feet is in the same order as in skating with ice or roller skates, except that on skis the strides are taken much more slowly. One ski is edged sharply on the inside edge and the skier pushes off briskly from that ski at an angle of about 30° on the other ski, at the same time giving a strong backward push with both poles. The first ski is lifted bodily, the tip coming out of the snow first to prevent the ski's dragging in the snow and causing a fall. The raised ski is kept in the air in preparation for the next step. A long slide with the weight well over the gliding ski should be secured. Near the end of the glide, the skier slowly edges the gliding ski in preparation for pushing off from it on the next glide. This sequence is followed alternately on each ski. The skating stride should not be a mere spasmodic picking up of alternate skis and a subsequent struggle for balance, but should be done slowly and forcefully.

Figure 52. Skating stride.

Since the skier is on one ski at a time, balance is poor. Yet it is this very lack of balance which makes the skating stride valuable practice. The ability to run confidently on one ski is well worth attaining, for the skier may often find himself momentarily and unexpectedly on one ski, and should feel at home there.

38. Pole Riding.

On narrow trails and steep slopes, the choice of ways of reducing speed is limited. Pole riding (fig. 53) is a simple and effective method. The poles can be used in two different positions:

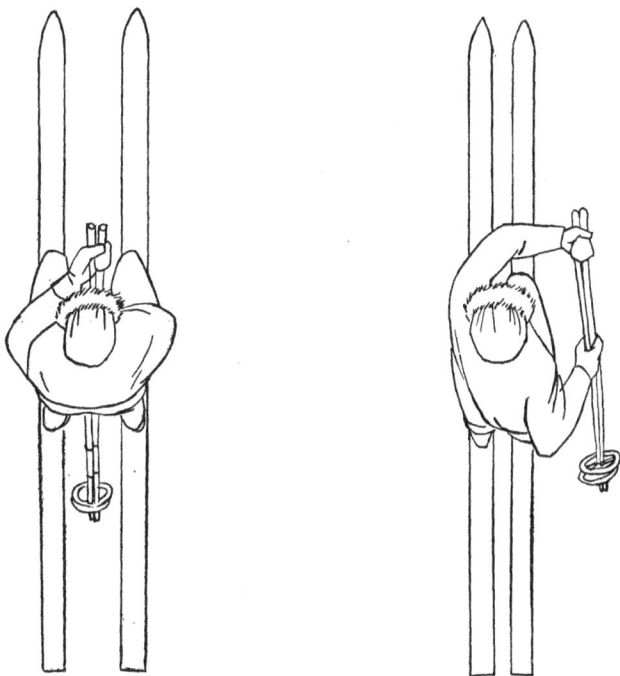

Figure 53. Pole riding.

a. Together and to the Rear between the Legs. Skis are a foot or so apart, and the rings of the poles drag on the snow. Increased friction with the snow is obtained by placing one hand on the handles of the poles, and other hand partway down the poles pushing them into the snow.

b. Together and on either Side of the Body. The rings are dragged in the snow on the uphill side, the necessary pressure being applied by the uphill hand at a point midway on the poles.

39. Jump Turns.

a. The use of jump turns (fig. 54) permits the skier to turn where there is too little space for a curved turn, or where the snow texture is so poor that an ordinary turn would be too difficult. Jump turns are made only at low speeds, and with much the same motions as are used when putting both hands on a rail and vaulting over it. From a traversing position the soldier crouches low, and plants both poles in the snow near the tip of the lower ski. The jump is made inward and slightly forward to bring all the weight over the poles, where it is supported while the knees are lifted to bring the skis clear of the snow. At the same time the skis are pivoted around the poles and dropped into the snow pointing in the new direction and as near to the poles as possible. If they are dropped too far down the slope from the poles, a fall into the hill is likely to result. The poles should give adequate support and make it unnecessary to hurry the turn. In fact, the more the turn feels as if it were being done in slow motion, the steadier it is likely to be. The feeling is one of falling forward and downhill over the poles, which provide support just long enough for the skis to swing around to the slope below. The arms are kept stiff to aid in this vaulting movement.

Figure 54. Jump turns.

b. The jump turn may also be made with the inside pole alone, the hand pressing down on the strap as in ordinary walking. Since in this method the hands and poles are in the normal position for running, the turn may be made on shorter notice and at greater speed than the two–pole jump turn. However, there can be less support from one pole than from two, and since less weight can be placed on the pole, there will sometimes be more difficulty in getting skis out of the snow in the jump, and all motions must be made faster. In the one–pole jump turn, the skier does not try to jump too far around the turn; that is, when the jump is completed his feet should be about in line with the previously made track. If he does not wish to stop with the jump, then he jumps farther around the turn, but he must be sure the weight is well forward when he lands.

Section VII. TOWING SKIERS

40. General.

a. The mobility of units mounted on skis can be greatly increased by towing behind vehicles. Personnel on skis may also be towed behind horses for short distances.

b. The vehicle best suited for towing is the cargo carrier. This means of locomotion is practicable on any beaten or plowed track. On such terrain speeds up to 30 miles per hour can be maintained without fatigue or danger to the personnel being towed. Speeds up to 15 miles per hour can be maintained on slopes up to 15 degrees where unpacked snow does not exceed 18 inches in depth. It is not a practicable method in deep snow where slopes must be traversed.

c. Where more than three basic units of men are to be transported it is desirable to have one unloaded cargo carrier break trail.

41. Method of Towing.

a. The basic unit for towing on skis should be eight men (fig. 55) . Equipment needed is 120 feet of climbing rope for an eight man unit. This rope is passed through the towing lug of the vehicle, two 60-foot lengths extending to the rear.

b. The skiers place themselves at equal distances to the rear, four men to each rope, the last man on each rope at the extreme end of the rope. The skiers place themselves on the outside of the rope. Each man ties a butterfly knot in the rope. The ski poles are then passed through the loop at the butterfly knot, handles to the rear and baskets securing the poles to the loop. The skiers grasp the handles of the ski poles in each hand and assume the downhill running position. There should be at least 7 feet between the heels of the skis of the lead man and the tips of the skis of the man following. The first skier in line should be at least 14 feet in the rear of the towing vehicle.

c. The equipment of the towed unit should be carried in the vehicle.

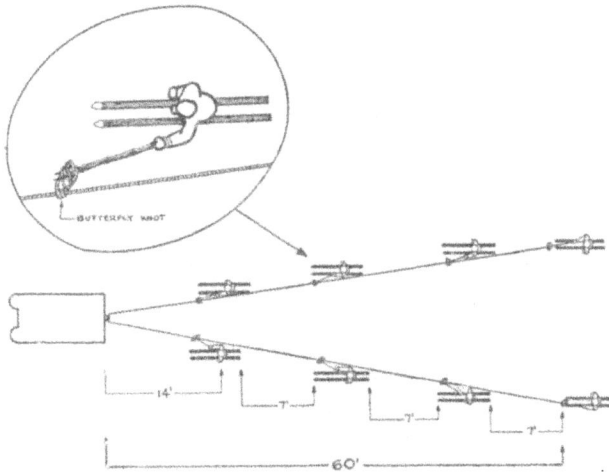

Figure 55. Towing skiers.

207

Section VIII. USE OF SKIS IN COMBAT

42. Methods of Dropping and Rising.

a. At the command DOWN, the man throws himself down in the most convenient manner. He may throw himself prone, with the legs outspread, the tips of the skis pointing outward; or he may throw himself on his right or left side, the skis parallel. It is imperative in dropping that neither weapons nor equipment be damaged, and that snow does not enter the muzzles of weapons. At the command UP, the soldier rises quickly and stands at ease.

b. When a man is heavily loaded, he should take great care to avoid falls. Falls with heavy packs waste strength, may render weapons unusable, and frequently lead to injuries. If a soldier cannot avoid falling while running downhill, he should throw himself diagonally backward. When rising, he should place his skis parallel in order to gain a firm position immediately after rising. On a slope, he should place his skis across the slope.

c. If, in falling, the skis get stuck in the snow, or a man sustains physical injuries, it is usually advisable for him to undo the bindings before rising. Troops must be able to strap and unstrap skis quickly, even when lying down. It is each man's duty to assist any other man who has suffered a hard fall.

43. Individual Combat Training.

a. WORKING FORWARD ON SKIS. (1) (Fig. 56.) The manner of advancing and the handling of skis in combat are influenced by the situation, the terrain, and the conditions of the snow. Methods other than those described in this manual may be used. When advancing by rushes, the soldier rises from the prone position and supports himself on his left knee. He holds the rifle vertically with the right hand and gives himself additional support by leaning with his left hand on the poles, which are kept together flat on the ground. He then draws up his right foot, sets the right ski in the desired direction, and starts to advance in a crouching position, pushing himself along with the rifle and the poles. While rushing forward, he keeps the rifle in his right hand and the poles in his left. The carbine, submachine gun, or automatic rifle are held similarly.

Figure 56. Rising from prone position.

(2) (Fig. 57.) When the soldier must slide forward in a prone position, he places his skis close together, lies with his stomach on the bindings, and slides forward by pushing himself with his hands. He may also push with his toes. When this method of advancing is used, the poles are placed on the skis, with the handles under the bindings and the snow rings on the ski tips. The rifle is either slung over the shoulder or laid on the skis in front of the soldier.

Figure 57. Advancing prone on skis.

209

(3) In deep, loose snow the soldier may advance by running in a crouching position. He slings his rifle horizontally in front of him, around his neck (fig. 58). The skis are placed parallel on the ground, separated by the width of his body, and the snow rings of the poles are placed on the skis

Figure 58. Advancing at crouch.

Figure 59. Advance over snow unsuitable to skiing.

at the bindings. Bending low and running, he grasps the ski bindings and poles together for support. If the terrain and the combat situation do not permit this method of advancing, the soldier goes down on his elbows and knees and pushes himself forward with his knees. The skis he moves forward one at a time, alternately, with his hands. If the condition of the snow is bad, the skis may be trailed while the soldier walks or rushes (fig. 59). He carries the rifle with the right hand, and with the left trails the skis, which are placed on top of each other. The poles may be carried in any convenient manner.

(4) Skis may be dragged while crawling, or even when advancing by other methods, by means of a cord which is put through the holes in the ski tips and fastened to the belt (fig. 60).

Figure 60. Crawling, dragging skis.

b. POSITIONS AND FIRING. (1) Usually only small units, such as patrols and raiding parties, will go into combat with their skis on. When snow and terrain are unfavorable, even small units take off their skis and fight on foot. A sudden encounter with the enemy, however, may temporarily require even a large unit to engage in a fire fight before the skis can be removed. FM 7–10 will serve as a general guide for the selection of an individual firing position, and for the conduct of a soldier with skis on while in a given position. In snow-covered terrain, camouflage against aerial and ground observation requires special care. By pressing his body into

211

the snow, the rifleman can conceal himself effectively.

(2) The various firing positions assumed by troops on skis depend on the terrain and the depth of the snow. Raising the muzzle slightly whenever the weapon is moved in the firing position will prevent snow from entering the unprotected barrel. Care must be taken to avoid the loss of ammunition and other small objects in the snow.

(3) In assuming the prone position, the soldier lies down toward the front with his legs outspread, the tips of the skis pointing outward. The rucksack,

Figure 61. Firing, prone, poles inserted in snow.

Figure 62. Firing, prone, poles on snow surface.

the snowshoes, or the crossed ski pole can serve as a rifle rest. When ski poles are used, the handles are pushed deeply into the snow and the points are crossed through the snow rings (fig. 61). The poles may also be placed horizontally on the snow to serve as an elbow rest (fig. 62). When the skis are removed from the feet, they may be used for the same purpose.

(4) In the kneeling position the left ski is placed half a pace forward. The soldier kneels on the right ski, the tip of which is pointed outward at an angle of approximately 45 degrees, and supports the rifle by placing his left arm on his left knee (fig. 63). It is easier to assume this position if the left ski is somewhat higher than the right one. If the bindings have a strong down pull, the kneeling position can be assumed only by placing the right ski to the rear. The rifleman lowers his right leg so that the foot and ankle lie on the snow and the

Figure 63. Firing, kneeling.

ski is turned up on edge. The crossed poles, held firmly together by the loops, constitute a rifle rest which is suitable for all variations of the kneeling position (fig. 64). The poles must be solidly placed in the snow.

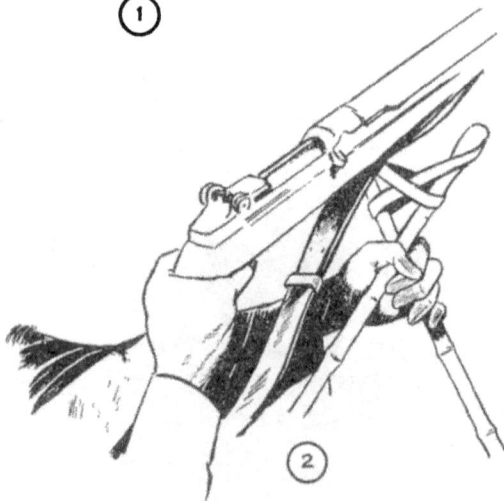

Figure 64. Use of poles when firing, kneeling.

(5) In the standing position (fig. 65), the tip of the right ski is moved about 45° to the right and the left ski advanced half a pace. The poles remain hanging from the wrists by the loops, but the left one is planted vertically into the snow and, supporting the left hand, serves as a rifle rest.

Figure 65. Firing, standing.

(6) The soldier mounted on skis may also fire from the squatting position. The tips of the skis are brought together, the heels pressed out at an angle of 15°. The skier faces obliquely to the right of his target, squats, and pivots to bring his weapon on the target. The inside edges of the skis are pressed into the snow. This position is dry, and very steady. It can be assumed rapidly.

(7) For firing from the prone position with the light machine gun, the snowshoe is the most practical base for the bipod (fig. 66). The bipod will be

firmer if the legs of the bipod are fastened tightly to the binding of the snowshoe. Thus the snowshoe will remain fastened to the bipod on the march as well as in combat. Other improvised rests, such as the rucksack and pine branches, may also be used, depending on the situation.

Figure 66. Firing a light machine gun.

c. USE OF GRENADES. Hand grenades are thrown as prescribed in FM 23–30, modified as may be necessary by the existing conditions. They may be thrown from the standing, kneeling, squatting, or prone positions.

d. CLOSE COMBAT. (1) In close combat the mobility of a man on skis is limited. Therefore, the skis are usually taken off before engaging in close fighting. They will be brought forward later by men designated for the purpose so that they will be readily available for continuing the attack or for pursuit.

(2) To exploit favorable momentary situations, however, it may sometimes be advisable to engage in close combat on skis. For this purpose, the poles are slipped under the belt to free the hands for handling weapons. Sometimes the poles themselves may be used as weapons.

e. DEPLOYMENT. The considerable marching depth of the platoon in single file impairs readiness for action. Therefore, when approaching enemy, deployment on a broad front takes place earlier than when marching without skis. In order to take advantage of the terrain however, and in order to reduce the number of tracks, the squad should remain in file as long as possible. As a rule, the platoon leader, with platoon headquarters, follows behind the leading squad. He may temporarily go to the point of the platoon for reconnaissance purposes, or he may move freely to the various points along the route which afford observation.

44. Combat Methods.

a. LEADERSHIP. (1) Poor skiers and soldiers not familiar with winter conditions are not suited as squad leaders of ski units.

(2) The peculiarities of the employment of ski troops require that the squad or platoon leader have special aptitude as a leader of scouting patrols, raiding parties, and other such independent missions. He must be specially trained, therefore, in orientation in open terrain and in carrying out marches on skis.

(3) He must also be familiar with the employment of, and cooperation with, heavy weapons units, with the handling and care of weapons and equipment in snow and cold, with the duties of engineer troops, and particularly with the construction of improvised shelters. Knowledge of first aid for wounds and frostbite, as well as protection against cold, is required of every subordinate leader.

b. CHARACTERISTICS OF COMBAT ON SKIS. (1) In combat on skis, the swift execution of all movements on the battlefield and the ability to deceive and outwit the enemy in every situation play a great part and greatly increase the striking power of even small units.

(2) In planned raids skis are used only as a means of locomotion. Fighting is done on foot. Upon arrival at the location of the enemy installation to be raided ski troops deploy, dismount. If the depth of snow permits, strike from different directions, withdraw in different directions, mount skis, fan out and rendezvous at predetermined assembly point.

(3) Squads and platoons frequently are specially organized and reinforced with heavy weapons and signal and engineer equipment to enable them to accomplish missions independently. Care must be taken that the mobility of the unit is not thereby impaired. Pieces of equipment which might reduce speed must be left behind or deposited during the approach march at selected points on the terrain.

(4) When approaching the enemy, advantage should be taken of poor visibility, such as fog, snow squalls, twilight, and darkness. Creeping skillfully and without a sound toward the enemy is of decisive importance in gaining a quick and thorough success. Close contact must be maintained within the squad and platoon.

(5) During attack and pursuit, envelopment should always be sought by utilizing mobility. Only weak forces should be left in front to deceive and pin down the enemy.

(6) If an attack bogs down in snowy terrain shortly before the objective is reached, heavy casualties usually result. Therefore, a decision must be sought as soon as possible and with the greatest tenacity. In choosing the direction of an attack, consideration must be given to the fact that difficult skiing terrain frequently offers better possibilities for a surprise breakthrough than favorable skiing terrain.

(7) Frontal assault uphill and in deep snow will

result in heavy casualties. Small units should be deployed as bases of fire with the major effort directed to the flank or rear. Flanking attacks should be launched from high ground whenever possible.

(8) Close combat is usually decided by the use of small arms and grenades. If possible, close combat should be started with a surprise attack; if on skis, by a rapid downhill run. It may be more practical in certain instances to avoid meeting the enemy in hand-to-hand combat and to seek a decision through a fire fight within the most effective range.

(9) By equipping troops with skis it is possible to conduct a mobile and aggressive defense. Ski troops must be utilized to a particularly great extent against an enemy who is not equipped with skis and whose mobility is limited.

c. THE FIRE FIGHT. Fire fights of the infantry in snow-covered terrain take on added importance because the terrain can be kept under observation more easily and also because visibility is usually better. In cases where ski troops have no artillery support, fire fights alone are frequently the only means of securing the success of the engagement. Increasing the allotment of telescopic sights to riflemen strengthens the effective fire power of the squad and favors the more frequent firing of single shots. Concentration of the fire of all rifles with telescopic sights to overpower important single targets (enemy leaders, observation posts, and machine guns) can be of particular advantage before and during an attack, and also in defense. Because of the limitations of transportation in ski warfare the platoon or squad.leader must control the use of ammunition.

d. SECURITY FOR A RESTING COMMAND (fig. 67). (1) Ski troops frequently fight alone, independent of larger units. Such tactics require special security measures and increased watchfulness on the part of all troops employed as security patrols. At night and with poor visibility, in terrain which is difficult to observe and is near the enemy, all normal security measures must be increased. Men should always be assigned to patrol and sentry duty in pairs. The leader charged with maintaining security will decide whether sentries and patrols shall move on skis or on foot. Sentries at fixed posts must be camouflaged day and night.

(2) Long hours of guard duty in any weather, particularly after strenuous marches, are part of the training of every ski unit and must also be required of all members of supply columns. The necessity for constant supervision and care of sentries and patrols by the squad or platoon leader is greatly increased during operations in extreme cold.

(3) To provide immediate security for quarters located near the enemy, a circular ski track may be made. This is established, depending on the situation and the terrain, at a radius of 1,000 to 1,500 yards around the position, in a manner permitting observation of enemy terrain. The track, however, should be concealed as much as possible. Sentries are established in heated tents, sheds, or farmhouses at the roadside or other points important for the protection of the position. Old tracks, extending beyond the security circle should either be properly marked or be obliterated. Patrols and runners should cross the security circle only on previously designated and marked tracks passing near the outguards. Patrols from the supports of the outposts guard the security track by constantly circulating on it.

(4) If new tracks of unknown origin are discovered, patrols will investigate and, if necessary, alert

the outpost. A second narrower track may be constructed around the quarters and guarded in a similar manner to provide close-in protection.

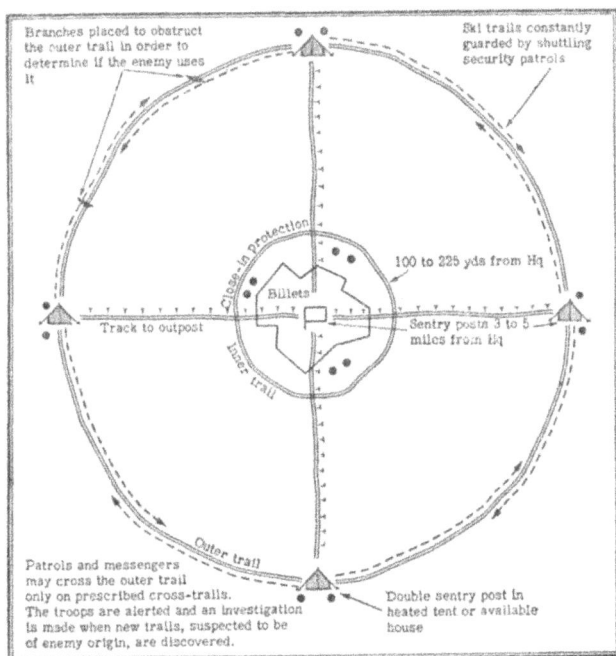

Figure 67. Diagram of security posts.

(5) Tracks for messengers must permit speedy skiing, and it must be possible to find them without difficulty even in the dark and in foggy weather. Snow squalls require frequent renewal of the tracks. In extreme cold, special trails for ski or foot travel should be prepared in the immediate vicinity of the sentries to give them an opportunity to warm up by vigorous movements. Sentries should be relieved at short intervals.

221

(6) To increase security and to protect sentries and outguards, various simple obstacles and alarms should be constructed on tracks or communication roads leading toward the enemy. Trip wires hidden in the snow and connected with mines, booby traps, or alarm mechanisms are particularly useful.

(7) Listening posts are especially important at night in snow covered terrain, and also in daytime, if the position is defiladed. At night, patrols, sentries, and outguards should be equipped with flare pistols and an ample supply of flares. Regardless of the protection provided by circular ski tracks, reconnaissance by patrols in the direction of the enemy must be continuous.

45. Mobility and Transportation.

a. The employment of heavy infantry weapons in a ski unit depends generally on the means of transportation available and the degree of mobility which is possible. Heavy weapons must be mobile to such an extent that they can follow the ski unit even off trails and roads. A few mobile heavy weapons with an adequate supply of ammunition are generally more useful than many weapons which lack mobility and for which ammunition supply is difficult or impossible.

b. Cargo carriers, hand sleds, and toboggans are the best means of transportation for heavy weapons that can be dismantled, such as heavy machine guns, 81-mm mortars, antitank guns, and 75-mm pack howitzers. The ammunition for these weapons should also be loaded on cargo carriers, hand sleds, or toboggans.

c. Weapons of great weight which cannot be dismantled are loaded on troughs, or cargo sleds and are hauled by horses or tracked vehicles.

46. Employment and Effectiveness.

a. HEAVY MACHINE GUN. The fundamentals of the employment of the heavy machine gun remain essentially unchanged. Observation of fire, preparation of the position, and adjustment of fire in snow-covered terrain require special training. Employment from a camouflaged position will be possible only in exceptional cases. Firing over our own troops is permitted only if the gun mount is resting on a firm base. However, it usually becomes necessary to substitute the light machine gun for the heavy machine gun.

b. 81-MM MORTAR. The 81-mm mortar is the most important high-angle weapon of the ski unit. It can be carried on a pack-board by snowshoers, or transported on hand sleds. Adjustment of fire usually requires a larger amount of ammunition than is needed under normal conditions. In low temperatures the weapon at first fires somewhat short; therefore, adjustment of fire should be started at a greater range than that originally calculated. Fragmentation of mortar ammunition decreases in deep snow. A correspondingly higher expenditure of ammunition is therefore to be expected. If the snow is thin or frozen over, mortar shells with superquick fuzes are particularly effective. Mortar shells must be cleared of snow before they are inserted in the barrel. It is advisable to leave the tube brush in the barrel until shortly before firing so that particles of snow and ice will be removed when the brush is withdrawn.

c. ANTITANK WEAPONS. (1) 57-mm and 37-mm antitank guns can be used by ski troops anywhere that tanks can operate. Where these weapons cannot be transported behind vehicles or animals they can be moved for considerable distances off roads and over rugged terrain by hand with the help of ropes and tackle.

(2) In winter operations the rocket launcher and the antitank grenade, because of their comparative mobility, will normally be the most effective antitank protection.

d. CALIBER .50 MACHINE GUNS. The caliber .50 machine gun can be easily transported and can be used for protection against aircraft or against lightly armored vehicles.

47. The Trail-breaking Detachment.

a. MISSIONS, COMPOSITION, AND EQUIPMENT. (1) Every unit must be thoroughly trained in trail-breaking and must practice it in any weather, at any time of day, and in all conditions of snow. A trail-breaking detachment is formed only if the unit is of platoon strength or larger, and is employed to break trails in deep, soft, and trackless snow in order to facilitate the advance of its parent unit. If snowshoe troops are available, they can be used to break trail, two snowshoers walking abreast. If the situation does not permit the employment of such a detachment, the unit must break its own trail. In easy terrain and under normal conditions, the trail may also be broken by road reconnaissance units.

(2) The trail-breaking detachment is divided into several trail-breaking details, the number of which depends on the number of tracks to be cut. One trail-breaking detail is designated as the guiding detail and the others follow in echelon. A trail-breaking detail usually consists of a leader and 6 to 10 men.

(3) The trail-breaking detachment of a company will normally consist of one or two details; that of a battalion, one or two platoons. When

snow is heavy and the weather is bad, the detachment should be doubled. The number of tracks to be made depends on the composition of the column, as well as on the strength and composition of the unit which follows. Ski tracks can be used for cargo sleds, or special sled trails may be cut by unloaded snow tractors.

(4) The lead which the detachment must have depends on the situation, the condition of the snow, and the weather. In general, it will be about ½-hour for each 3 miles. The detachment, in addition to cutting tracks, removes small obstacles, employing wire cutters, hatchets, brush knives, spades, and other tools. Its personnel must carry only minimum loads.

(5) When operating in the vicinity of the enemy, the trail-breaking detachment acting as the point also provides security for the parent unit. The nearer the approach to the enemy the greater the emphasis on security and the less the emphasis on trail-breaking functions. It must be ready for defensive action, even if reconnaissance patrols have been sent ahead. Reinforcement of the detachment with light machine-gun crews, automatic riflemen, and riflemen may be advisable.

b. FUNCTION OF LEADERS. (1) The leader of the trail-breaking detachment is to be instructed in his duties personally by the commander of the parent unit. The mission must include definite instructions concerning the route (its azimuth should be given on a map, or it should be pointed out on the terrain), the number and type of required trails, the objective, the intended rest areas, and the measures to be taken when meeting the enemy and after the mission has been accomplished. Furthermore, the leader is to be informed of the intelligence and reconnaissance measures taken in connection with the execution of his mission.

(2) The leader of the trail-breaking detachment ment organizes the column, designates the guiding detail, specifies the azimuth, the intervals between the details and their special equipment, and the positions for himself and his assistant.

(3) The guiding detail cuts the main trail and is usually in the middle of the formation. If the route follows roads, railroads, and deep cuts, a different detail may be assigned the guide functions. If the detachment has hand sleds, they usually follow in the main trail behind the reserve detail. The leader of the detachment remains with the guiding detail, accompanied by one or two messengers. He does not participate in the actual work of breaking trail.

c. BREAKING TRAIL. (1) A trail should be broken out in as simple a manner as the terrain permits. The requirements of the unit which follows and not the convenience of those who are cutting the trail are the important factors. Since even minor obstacles can retard the march considerably, they should be by-passed as often as possible. It must be remembered that uphill tracks become more slippery as they are used. Brush, straw, or similar materials should be placed over wet spots so that the troops can pass over them without getting their skis wet. If obstacles cannot be by-passed, several sets of tracks must be broken out over them so that units which follow can cross on a broad front. Multiple trails for a number of columns will facilitate route and approach march movement on skis. This method of movement should be considered normal for ski-equipped elements.

(2) To save energy, uphill trails should have as few turns as possible. Slopes should be uniform

and adapted to the poorest skier. On curves, skis are not to be raised off the ground. They must be slid on the snow into the desired direction.

(3) Unloaded cargo carriers are useful in breaking trails.

(4) For short distances, a usable path for cargo sleds can be made by packing the snow. This may be done effectively by a detail on snowshoes, but is better done by power equipment. When large units are marching, it is advisable to break out a separate trail for line-of-communication traffic. It is advisable to lay it directly alongside the main trail.

(5) Snowfalls obliterate tracks within a short time. It then becomes necessary to send the trail-breaking detachment ahead with only a slight start or to send a second detachment to renew the trail just before beginning the ski march.

(6) The mileage covered by the trail-breaking detachment depends on the terrain, vegetation, and character of snow. Except under unusual conditions, the detachment can break the trail for a day's march of a large ski unit. To maintain endurance and to guarantee an uninterrupted march, the leading men of the trail-breaking details must be regularly relieved. In very deep and heavy snow, a relief may become necessary every 300 feet. When the change is ordered, the man to be relieved steps sideways out of the tracks and falls in at the end of the column, while the man following him becomes the point. Special equipment is exchanged. In a well-trained ski unit the soldiers assigned as leading men relieve one another even without specific orders. Under difficult conditions, it may be advisable to relieve the whole guide detail from time to time with a reserve detail.

d. MARKING THE TRAILS. (1) Each trail-breaking detachment should mark its trail as uniformly as possible. The types of markings to be used must be known to the unit that follows. When several details are operating, the marking of the trail cut by the guiding detail is usually sufficient. The marking should be simple, but recognizable by night as well as by day. For tracks in new snow which will be used only once or only temporarily, it is sufficient, where other tracks or roads are crossed, to erect unobtrusive markers. Trails which are intended for frequent use over a long period must be marked more permanently.

(2) The following may be used as trail-markers:

(a) Distinct signs in the snow (for instance, three impressions with the snow ring of the ski pole, close together).

(b) Twigs on trees and shrubs broken in a predetermined manner.

(c) Poles or guiding arrows planted in the snow.

(d) Markers made of rags or colored paper.

(3) Snowfalls, fog, and poor observation necessitate especially thorough and frequent trail-marking. Orientation is facilitated if the markers are numbered successively in the direction of march and spaced at uniform intervals.

(4) Road markers, which can be erected quickly, may be used as effective road markers over wide, flat terrain unbroken by vegetation.

(5) In order to avoid the destruction or obliteration of trail-markers by traffic, the markers should be placed about three feet off the trail. When strange tracks cross the trail of the unit, they must be obliterated at the point of crossing. It may frequently be advisable to post sentries at crossings to direct units that follow.

(6) If a section of the route is under enemy observation or can be used only at certain times or

under certain conditions (for instance, with great intervals between men, or without cargo sleds) a sign must be erected at a suitable spot in front of the vulnerable section of the route with the necessary information, such as "Enemy observation within 300 feet; passable only after dark."

(7) The prompt removal of all trail-markers after the route has been used must be enforced.

48. March Formations.

a. Single file is the usual march formation of the ski unit. In order to shorten the depth of the file, which is four to six times the depth of a unit marching on foot, platoons should, whenever possible, march in several parallel sets of tracks. Companies and larger units will always do this, and their sections with cargo sleds will march as close together as possible on a single trail.

b. The approach march formation will be determined exclusively on the basis of tactical considerations. The formation of a march column on a large scale requires detailed orders. This is particularly important when marching in heavy snow and bad weather as well as in darkness and cloudy weather. The relief of units marching at the head of the column is necessary from time to time.

c. If sufficient engineer forces are not already with the reconnaissance squads, engineers should be incorporated and placed at the head of the column, adequately equipped with tools for the removal of obstacles. At the end of each column, reserve skis as well as spare parts and repair tools must be carried on hand sleds, if possible. If packed roads are available, cargo sleds may use them while the skiers march on several sets of tracks on the adjoining open terrain. Skiers must be detailed to protect each sled echelon that is marching independently and to aid the sled crews at difficult places.

49. March Security.

a. Normal security measures will be adequate for men on skis. Units detailed for other purposes (breaking trails, reconnaissance) also share in security tasks.

b. Over snow and in cold, noises carry long distances. Therefore, any unnecessary noise must be avoided during the march. For each column and each squad on the march, certain skiers should be detailed to stop frequently at the side of the road to listen for noises indicating enemy activity. Flank and rear guards should be kept as mobile as possible and should not be equipped with hand sleds or toboggans. It will frequently be necessary for flank patrols to start before the trail-breaking units. When visibility is good, security units advance in bounds from one point of observation to another. When difficult terrain and bad weather interfere with the maintenance of a secure system of communication by means of messengers on skis, it may be necessary to equip security units with radio equipment.

c. On the approach of enemy aircraft, the skiers leave the trail and disperse, taking cover by crouching and supporting themselves with their arms on the skis. They remain motionless in this position until the all-clear. Cargo sleds remain on the trail and the drivers stay with them. All riflemen and machine-gun crews take part in the defense against low-flying air attack. To deceive enemy air observers, it may be advisable to employ a special detail to obliterate the tracks left behind by the column. This precaution is especially important when entering woods and villages and when leaving billets.

50. March Discipline.

a. The march pace must not be allowed to slacken on slight uphill slopes, and the troops must not bunch up at the start or finish of a downhill stretch but must continue the march at the normal pace. Obstacles must be negotiated on the broadest possible front without slackening the speed of the march. Special training of pace setters is important.

b. Troops marching close to sleds will promptly help to push sleds over obstacles without waiting for orders. When crossing frozen bodies of water whose carrying capacity for loaded cargo sleds seems doubtful the sleds are unloaded; troops will then haul the sleds across the ice surface. Units in the rear must be warned of difficult sections of the road which require special attention. This can be done by erecting suitably worded sign, by passing back a message from man to man, or by posting a sentry.

c. It is advisable to halt briefly after crossing a large obstacle in order to close up the column and to check for stragglers. In every unit on the march, one man (if possible, an officer or noncommissioned officer) should be detailed as end man to supervise march discipline. If a man must fall out, he immediately clears the tracks by stepping aside and reports to the second-in-command at the rear of the column, who tells him how to continue the march. If the man will be delayed for a long period, a second man must always be detailed to accompany him. The same procedure is followed when sleds fall behind.

d. Where units are moving in multiple columns the interval between parallel columns will depend on terrain, communication, and the tactical situation. In special situations where good routes are widely separated and speedy movement is essential, continuous lateral contact may be relaxed, but units must maintain control by making contact at successive march objectives.

51. Rest.

a. After about 15 minutes of marching, a short halt of 5 minutes is ordered for straightening out ski bindings and hand sleds, adjusting packs, and removing excess clothing. During such a halt the skis remain on the feet and the sleds stay in the trail. The frequency of rest periods depends on the situation, the snow, the weather, the availability of tactically suitable resting places, and the degree of fatigue of the troops. Unless it is planned to eat, or to serve hot drinks, the rest should not last longer than 5 minutes. Small units on separate missions may often find that long slow marches with infrequent rests (5 minutes every 1½ hours) are best. A proper pace and easy route to reach successive selected march objectives are command responsibilities.

b. In extreme cold and biting wind, efforts should be made to accomplish the march without rest. Under such conditions, rest periods do no good and easily cause colds. Villages, woods, underbrush, and depressions sheltered from the wind, which offer sufficient concealment against ground and air observation and can easily be guarded, are the most suitable rest sites. If possible, water should be nearby and resting places should be selected some distance from the track. If the rest is to last several hours, the possibility of ordering a bivouac must be considered. Units should be directed to the resting site by means of signs or sentries.

c. The skis are taken off during a rest period only when the leader of the unit orders it. When the temperature is below freezing and the skis are removed, they must be placed on the snow with the running surfaces down. During a thaw, the skis should be planted in the snow, heels down, and snow must be kept off the running surfaces. If necessary, skis may be rewaxed during long stops.

d. When the situation requires a long halt, warm drinks should be served. All tracks made during a halt must be obliterated as effectively as possible, in order to avoid giving clues to enemy air and ground reconnaissance. The march is resumed at a moderate pace which is accelerated gradually to normal marching speed. To prevent perspiration clothing should be removed on the march, stripping to the waist if necessary. If troops are perspiring freely on a march in cold weather, the pace should be slowed toward the end of the march to permit a gradual cooling off and drying of dampened clothes.

Section IX. PATROLS, ASSAULT TROOPS, AND RAIDING PARTIES

52. Missions.

a. The ski patrol is the most important reconnaissance organization in snow-covered terrain. It may be employed for detailed reconnaissance as well as general reconnaissance. Its mission may sometimes last several days.

b. Because of its mobility the ski patrol is particularly fitted to execute, besides reconnaissance, minor combat missions to harass the enemy. Detachments on skis which are organized for the sole purpose of executing limited combat missions are designated as ski assault troops.

c. A raiding party is used chiefly for the demolition or destruction of distant objectives or for missions behind enemy lines. It must be able to accomplish combat missions independently, fighting for several days without reliance on the supply installations of the main unit. In particular, raiding parties may be employed:

(1) To conduct reconnaisance in force over large areas.

(2) To destroy enemy artillery positions, to annihilate troops and reserves separated from their units, and to raid command posts.

(3) To destroy shelters, supply installations, and transport facilities.

(4) To intercept and destroy food or ammunition supply columns.

53. Strength, Composition, and Equipment.

a. The strength, composition, and equipment of ski patrols, assault troops, and raiding parties depend to a great extent on the mission, situation, and probable length of separation from the main unit. The guiding factors in selecting personnel for these ski groups are aggressiveness, marksmanship, and proficiency in skiing. Especially versatile officers or noncommissioned officers must be detailed as leaders. The assignment of a man who speaks the language of the enemy or of the local inhabitants is advantageous.

b. The usual strength of a ski patrol is one squad. For the accomplishment of certain missions, however, it may be larger and be reinforced with engineers and artillery observers. The assignment of a radio team is usually advisable.

c. The organization and equipment of the ski assault unit are based on the requirements of the mission. The strength of this unit varies between a squad and a platoon.

d. The strength of a raiding party ranges from a platoon up to a company. As a rule, heavy weapons and light antitank weapons are attached. The mobility of the raiding party, however, must not be impaired thereby. Heavy weapons loaded on hand sleds are generally preferable to those which can be moved only on cargo sleds. Assault guns or tanks may be attached to raiding parties.

e. In selecting equipment to be taken along, the aim must be to achieve the greatest possible economy in weight. The equipment which will permit the individual soldier to maintain his fighting strength must be based on the tactical requirements of the contemplated action. Written orders or maps with overlays which may be of value to the enemy must not be taken along.

f. Maximum fire power and mobility are decisive factors in determining the type and number of weapons with which the individual ski trooper should be equipped. Therefore, the men must be equipped with the largest possible number of automatic weapons, rifles with telescopic sights, and a correspondingly large supply of ammunition.

g. The number of heavy weapons to be taken along depends on the facilities for carrying sufficient ammunition. Fewer arms and plenty of ammunition should be the rule. The amount of rations, bivouac, signal and orientation equipment, pioneer and medical supplies, as well as ski repair equipment, depends mainly on the expected duration of the action. Prepared, nourishing foods, rich in fat (which, moreover, do not occupy much space and are not affected by weather conditions) will if possible be taken. Every third man is to be equipped with cooking gear. Cooking by small groups should be encouraged.

h. Bivouac equipment should always be taken along if bivouacs in the snow, outside villages, are expected. For actions in terrain without vegetation or inhabitants, fuel must be taken along. On his pack every man carries sleeping bag and warm windproof, and water-repellent clothing.

i. Larger patrols and raiding parties should be equipped with a radio of sufficient range for communication with the main unit. This equipment may be carried on a packboard, in a cargo carrier, or on a hand sled.

j. For purposes of orientation, it is necessary to take along compasses (at least two for each squad), binoculars, watches, and trail markers or material for improvising such markers (arrows, flags, paint, colored paper, and other articles).

k. Engineer equipment, such as explosives and mines, are taken along if the mission requires. An abundant supply of wire cutters, hatchets, spades, and hand saws is usually advisable. Medical equipment, carried on a hand sled suitable for transporting wounded men, consists mainly of bandages, antifrost materials, and stimulants.

l. It is indispensable, even for the smallest ski unit, to have ski repair equipment, including spare parts for bindings, spare tips for skis, and the necessary repair tools. For longer missions, it is also necessary to take along extra skis and poles.

54. Employment of Patrols, Assault Troops, or Raiding Parties.

a. GENERAL COMBAT PRINCIPLES. (1) Ski troops are the most mobile arm of the infantry in snow-covered terrain, and they are best utilized in combat away from roads. Because of their special training and equipment, ski troops can execute combat missions lasting several days without support from other forces and independent of supply from higher echelons.

(2) Skill in outwitting the enemy, courage, and a ruthlessly aggressive spirit are prime requisites for the success of ski patrols, assault units, and raiding parties. Fast action, in which the element of surprise is utilized, secures superiority, even against a far stronger enemy. In a surprise engagement with the enemy, to attack is almost always the right thing to do.

(3) The main principles of combat procedure are:

(a) To get off the roads into the snow, and approach the enemy cross-country.

(b) To get out of the villages and march through woods.

(c) To remain mobile.

(d) To capture and secure commanding heights.

(4) If the mission leads behind enemy lines, it is advisable to utilize the night or foggy weather in order to penetrate the outposts of the enemy. Through early reconnaissance it must be determined where openings in the enemy's defenses are located and where his flanks may be by-passed.

(5) Combat with numerically superior, equally mobile enemy units of similar type must be avoided. Envelopment or surprise by the enemy must be prevented by increased watchfulness.

(6) Every commitment demands the exact formulation of an operational plan by the leader. The plan and mission must be known to every member of the unit. In general, the plan must cover the following phases of the mission: route of march,

main track, conduct if contact is made with the enemy, execution of the specific mission, assembly after the mission has been accomplished, return to the main body.

b. THE APPROACH MARCH. (1) The approach march requires careful husbanding of strength to enable the unit to reach its objective in good physical condition. The return route, which should be different from that used in approaching the objective, will be designated during the approach march.

(2) On the march, ski patrols of squad strength break their own trails. They generally send scouts ahead. Raiding parties send out one of several trail-breaking details, which also provide security during the march. Marching on several parallel sets of track reduces the depth of the column and at the same time increases preparedness for combat. To save strength, it may be advantageous, in certain areas, to tow ski patrols and raiding parties behind horses or motor vehicles.

(3) Tracks of unknown origin must be treated with the greatest suspicion. They may have been prepared by the enemy and may be mined or may lead to an ambush.

(4) Small detachments may prevent the enemy from making an accurate estimate of their strength by ordering all men to insert their poles in the same places as the preceding men, or by keeping their poles raised in certain areas.

(5) The manner of carrying the weapons depends on the degree of readiness for combat which is necessary, and will be prescribed by the unit commander.

(6) The approach is made by bounds from observation point to observation point, using covered routes. If it is necessary to pass places which are subject to observation and which are particu-

larly dangerous during daylight, parts of the unit will be deployed to provide protection until the unit has passed. Then they will rejoin the unit as soon as possible. At night, silence in all movements is an important factor. The direction of the wind may be decisive in selecting a route of approach. In moonlight the march should follow a shadowed route as much as possible in order to provide concealment from the enemy.

(7) No forward movement should be made in mountainous territory until commanding heights in the vicinity have been secured.

(8) Within range of the enemy, it is necessary to decide whether skis should be kept on or stacked and how far hand sleds may go. In order to obtain cover and concealment, it is often necessary to use detours or terrain unfavorable for skiing. An attempt must be made at all times to gain, under cover, heights from which it will be possible to make a rapid descent through terrain which is under fire or observation.

c. TACTICS. (1) Combat and tactical measures depend on the mission and the enemy situation. Ski patrols on a reconnaissance mission fight only if it is necessary for the accomplishment of the mission, or if the situation is momentarily favorable.

(2) The missions of ski assault units and raiding parties generally require bold and sudden execution. The aim must be to give the enemy no rest at any time, to weaken and paralyze his fighting power, and to prevent him from using his numerical superiority. Skillful and versatile leadership may annihilate a much stronger enemy or at least inflict heavy losses on him. In woods and at night, small detachments may shake the morale of the enemy tremendously through mobile and surprise attacks.

Careful preparation and lightning action are the basis for success of all missions of this kind.

(3) The strength and location of the enemy as well as the terrain he occupies must be carefully reconnoitered before entering battle. Such reconnaissance, however, must not disclose the contemplated action to the enemy. An engagement will always be opened by surprise fire. The more suddenly it hits the enemy and the less he is able to take quick defensive measures, the more effective it will be. The sudden opening of surprise fire often results in complete annihilation of the enemy.

(4) To deceive the enemy with regard to the strength of the attacking unit, it may be practical to stage the attack on a broad front or with several detachments firing simultaneously from several directions. If possible, the combat position will be established in terrain which is unfavorable for hostile counterattack but which permits the ski unit to shift or withdraw under cover.

(5) Ski patrols, assault units, or raiding parties are not suited for a prolonged engagement, because of their usually limited ammunition supply. They detach themselves from the enemy after accomplishing their mission, or complete his destruction in close combat.

(6) Night is generally best for carrying out harassing missions. Darkness facilitates disengaging from the enemy after completion of a mission. The attack should be made from a direction that will facilitate the cutting of the enemy's communications with his rear. If sufficient forces are available, total encirclement of the enemy is most likely to succeed. If a mission has failed or only partially succeeded, the leader decides whether or not the mission will be continued, repeated at another point, or abandoned.

d. DISENGAGING ACTIONS. (1) Disengaging from the enemy is an essential part of operations and must be provided for in the operational plan of the leader of a ski patrol, assault unit, or raiding party. At times the return may prove more difficult than the approach.

(2) The method of evacuaion depends on the situation and terrain. It is carried out by a simultaneous withdrawal of all elements, or, in order to provide covering fires, a gradual withdrawal. In a gradual withdrawal the leader designates the men and weapons which remain in contact with the enemy, usually under his direction. As long as the raiding party is under fire, it will retreat, if possible, on previously prepared tracks made from one assembly point to another, as designated by the leader. Ski tracks often remain visible for a long time and betray the route. Therefore, the enemy must be deceived as to the return route by dummy tracks, loops, and false route signs.

(3) In newly fallen snow the tracks may be blurred by spruce branches dragged by the last skier. If the enemy pursues, as many delays as possible must be arranged for him. These include sudden fire from ambush, trail-breaking through difficult terrain, preparation of road blocks and obstacles, and mining of trails.

(4) If possible, ambush positions will be established on ridges from which it is possible to direct effective enfilading fire at the enemy during his slow ascent.

55. Operations.

a. RECONNAISSANCE AND SECURITY. (1) The ski unit, whose missions usually lead into unknown terrain and unreconnoitered situations, is in great danger of being surprised by the enemy. Unceasing reconnaissance and security efforts and an ever alert eye at all times and under all conditions are therefore prime requisites for all operations.

(2) Preparatory to the attack, reconnaissance will be made on a broad front in such a manner that the enemy cannot draw any conclusions as to the direction of the assault. Full advantage will be taken of every opportunity to deceive the enemy by pseudo-reconnaissance and by leading enemy observation and security into a wrong direction. Twilight and bright nights must be utilized for reconnaissance in the same manner as daylight.

(3) Well-camouflaged observers must supplement reconnaissance efforts within the range of their vision. In snow-covered terrain, the enemy cannot forever evade conscientious and thorough observation. Observation also contributes to the security of the unit in bivouac, on the march, and in combat.

(4) Information concerning winter road nets behind the enemy front is especially important, not only in determining the direction of our own assault but also that of the enemy. Reconnaissance of enemy terrain will therefore stress roads and trails available to the enemy, which must be marked on maps and road sketches.

(5) Safe transmission of orders and messages, and contact between patrols by means of identification and communication signals, must be regulated by order.

b. ATTACK. (1) In snow-covered terrain, a roadbound enemy will be hard hit by an attack against his flank and rear, and, above all, against his rear communications. Therefore, the enveloping attack, utilizing the mobility afforded by skis, is the most effective type of action for ski troops. Against an enemy who is already shaken or who is not prepared for defense, a bold frontal attack may also be successful.

(2) Moving into the assembly area may be expedited by cutting trails in advance. The units assigned to break trails also take over local security in the assembly area. For this purpose, they will be equipped with light machine guns. If the approach to the assembly area under cover is impossible, it may be advisable, in order to deceive the enemy or to cause him to split up his fire power, to trickle into the assembly area singly or in small groups at irregular intervals, each man breaking his own trail. This method, however, requires considerably more time and will be employed only if the weather permits a long stay in the area.

(3) Heavy infantry weapons and artillery pieces should be placed sufficiently forward at the beginning of the operation to enable them to support the attacking troops from their initial positions as long as possible. Because of the difficulty of moving them during combat, they will be placed in position as soon as practicable in accordance with the operational order. Rapid changes of position are facilitated by preparing tracks in advance to the new positions.

(4) The urge to speed the attack must not result in insufficient preparation. In determining time factors, it must be remembered that the emplacement of heavy weapons and the preparation for firing all weapons usually takes twice as long in deep snow and severe cold as under ordinary conditions. All preparations (reconnaissance of the assembly area and observation posts, locations of firing positions, breaking of trails, etc.) must therefore be started early.

(5) It may be advisable to echelon in depth in the assembly area the forces which are to carry out

an envelopment, or to give them an advantage in time at the beginning of the attack. To retain mobility, they must usually forego support by heavy weapons, but they must be amply equipped with automatic weapons. It is advisable to attach heavy weapons observers and, if the occasion arises, artillery observers.

(6) The time interval between the completion of the assembly and the beginning of the attack must be kept to a minimum, because lying around in cold and snow is extraordinarily weakening. Therefore, infantry always moves last into the assembly area.

(7) The time of attack should not always be the same, but should be changed frequently to deceive the enemy. Attacks at night or during periods of poor visibility are best to gain surprise and to minimize losses. They require, however, particularly careful preparation, including, if possible, daylight reconnaissance of the terrain and of enemy positions. Objectives of night attacks should not necessitate long approaches.

(8) Enveloping attacks should be executed with simultaneous reconnaissance in front and at the flank in order to enable the enveloping force to bypass the hostile flanks under maximum cover and to encircle the enemy completely. Bold and determined leadership and a high degree of protection for the flanks of the enveloping forces are the basis of success. The encirclement is further tightened by means of minor attacks from other directions; meanwhile, holding forces must be employed for defense against hostile attempts to relieve the pressure. A few squads armed with machine guns will usually suffice for this purpose. As the encirclement becomes tighter, it may be advisable to force the enemy to stage costly frontal

counterattacks in deep snow, or to whittle him down and destroy him by further systematic attacks. Automatic weapons are suitable for this purpose.

(9) An attack through defenses in depth should be subdivided into several successive stages, each with a short-range objective. Upon capture of each objective the unit should be reorganized and the attack against the next objective initiated.

c. PURSUIT. (1) The superiority of a well-trained ski unit is most effective in pursuit, and superior leadership can gain decisive successes by pursuit.

(2) A flanking pursuit over unguarded, pathless terrain, combined with direct pressure on the enemy on roads, is an effective combat technique. To increase mobility, some equipment, heavy weapons, and sleds must frequently be left behind. An effort must always be made during the pursuit to cut off the enemy from his route of retreat, enveloping him on both flanks and forcing him into a small area. As soon as the encircling ski troops are relieved by other troops, the ski units resume the pursuit on both sides of the route of retreat.

(3) The pursuit should be continued day and night, as long as possible. Numerous patrols should be continuously despatched in order to keep contact with the enemy, and, by means of ambushes and by blocking his routes of retreat, to inflict losses upon him constantly.

d. DEFENSE. (1) The basis of the power of the ski unit in defense is its operational mobility. The defender can prepare tracks for rapid movement throughout his position. The attacker is hampered by snow which renders him vulnerable to the rapidly shifting force of the defender. It is the responsibility of all commanders to retain mobility even during long periods of defensive action. When de-

245

fending on a broad front, strong reserves of ski assault troops, held ready for action, will take the place of a uniform and complete distribution of troops along the main line of resistance. The personnel and weapons of these reserves should be kept in warmth and shelter.

(2) The backbone of the defense will consist of strongpoints placed far to the front and suitable for all-around defense. Heavy weapons, with ample ammunition, should be emplaced in the strongpoints.

(3) Dummy installations, which are quickly and easily constructed in snow-covered terrain, will be employed in large numbers. Camouflage must be used to protect all changes in terrain, such as ski tracks and construction of shelters.

(4) Reconnaissance must be intensified when the front is broad and the strongpoints are few. Early recognition of enemy attacks, especially tank attacks, may be decisively important for successful defense. Tracks must be prepared in advance to make possible a quick change of the positions of heavy weapons.

(5) Frequent actions of ski assault units and raiding parties should be made against the front and the rear of the enemy to harry him, to weaken his power of resistance, and to force him to spread his forces thinly. At times, bold assaults can completely destroy enemy concentrations.

(6) To engage an enemy approaching or breaking into the main combat zone, battalion and company commanders hold in readiness reserve assault troops on skis for quick commitment along prepared tracks to the threatened position. Reserve troops should remain under cover in shelters or dugouts, if possible, in order that they may enter combat warm and rested.

(7) Counterattacks, when possible, should be directed against the flank of the attacking enemy, who must be annihilated with concentrated fire at close and point-blank range and in hand-to-hand combat. Especially effective is a pincer type counterattack, executed by several reserve assault columns for the purpose of encircling an enemy who has broken into the main battle position.

(8) In preparing plans for counterattacks, one must take into consideration the various possibilities for enemy attacks. The counterattacks must be rehearsed while in position.

e. WITHDRAWAL FROM ACTION. (1) Withdrawal from action is greatly facilitated by the mobility of ski troops and can often be carried out in daylight without particular danger. This is almost always possible if the position can be evacuated by means of a downhill run while the enemy is forced to reach the positions by a long climb. Tracks for the departure must be prepared beforehand.

(2) The order of withdrawal from positions depends on the mobility of the respective weapons. As a rule, the heavy weapons, loaded on sleds, are the first to be withdrawn and, if the situation permits, will be used from rearward positions to cover the retirement of troops remaining in position longest. Rallying positions should be prepared by advance detachments.

f. SUPPORT AND COOPERATION. (1) Only very limited employment of horse-drawn and motorized artillery by ski units can be made off the roads. To carry out a mission in which artillery support is advisable, single pieces will be mounted on runners and sleds to make them mobile enough to accompany ski troops, even over difficult terrain. Pack artillery and light antitank guns, dismantled and loaded on sleds, can follow the ski unit in any terrain where snow tractors can operate.

(2) If pack artillery, antitank guns, or other suitable light artillery are not available, the ski unit, as a rule, will have to dispense with artillery support unless the unit commander decides that the importance of such support justifies the reduction of the unit's mobility resulting from taking heavy guns along; or unless artillery support from advanced initial firing positions is possible.

(3) Because of the greater difficulties of observation over snow-covered terrain, to assure location of targets, it is necessary to detail additional advanced observers. In areas threatened by air attack, attachment of antiaircraft units to larger ski organizations will prove necessary. Their mobility, even off roads and prepared trails, must be assured by equipping them with sleds or runners.

(4) Assault-gun units are excellent for support of ski units if terrain and snow conditions are favorable. They can move through snow 12 inches deep without material loss of speed. If, however, the snow is deeper than the ground clearance of the vehicles (16 inches and up), their speed begins to decrease rapidly. Snow more than 29 inches deep cannot, as a rule, be negotiated by assault guns. When the snow is too deep, it may be necessary to use shovels in clearing approaches for such guns when they are employed in attacks with limited objectives.

(5) To conserve energy, assault guns may be used in suitable terrain to tow accompanying ski infantry. In an attack, the troops thus towed also furnish added local protection for the pieces.

(6) Assault-gun units require close cooperation and extensive support from the ski unit. In particular, engineers must be assigned for clearing

roads for the pieces, for removing mines, for early reconnaissance to determine snow depth, and the carrying capacity of bridges or of frozen bodies of water. Because of the difficulty of target recognition in snowy terrain, fire adjustment by accompanying infantry assumes increased importance.

(7) Attached tanks and assault guns will be employed normally, in platoon or company strength.

(8) The flexible employment of the ski unit requires thorough familiarity with ground-air liaison procedures. All members of the ski unit must be familiar with the meaning of the rules for, and the use of identification signals and codes between ground forces and air units.

(9) If a ski unit has penetrated deep into the enemy lines, it may be advantageous to indicate not only front lines but also flank and rear boundaries of the marching or fighting unit with panels, pyrotechnics and smoke signals. Support by aircraft in lieu of artillery, which is rarely available, assumes greater importance for ski units. Targets must be clearly designated by tracers and panels.

(10) Long-range missions may temporarily necessitate supply of the ski unit by airplanes. Panels for the place where supplies are to be dropped will be placed, wherever possible, in open terrain far enough away from the front line to conceal them from enemy ground observation, but plainly visible from the air. They must be removed promptly if enemy aircraft approaches.

g. COOPERATION WITH INFANTRY ON FOOT. (1) The ski unit can give considerable support to other infantry units because, being independent of roads, it may be committed quickly. It is the responsibility of the combined command to coordinate the commitment of the rapidly moving ski unit with the operations of the other units. The principles of combat and command of the ski unit are not changed when they are employed in combination with other units.

(2) Employment of the ski unit in this connection includes the following points:

(a) Reconnaissance and security measures over extensive areas.

(b) Screening of movements and security of friendly forces while they are assembling.

(c) Employment as flank and rear enveloping forces.

(d) Employment in pursuit and rear-guard actions.

(3) In missions within range of friendly artillery, operations of the ski unit can be considerably facilitated by artillery support.

h. ACTIONS BEHIND ENEMY LINES. (1) If a ski unit is ordered to perform a mission behind the enemy lines, it must first determine by reconnaissance of a broad front whether there is a gap in the enemy position through which it is possible to pass without detection, or whether it is possible to by-pass an enemy flank without engaging the enemy. As rule, missions of this type can be carried out only in darkness or foggy weather.

(2) If the enemy shows a solid front, it might become advisable for the ski unit to force its way through the enemy lines by systematic attack. To support this attack, the concentrated fire of artillery and all available heavy weapons not accompanying the ski unit should be utilized against the point selected for penetration, and also should be employed to screen the flanks. Depending on the circumstances, other parts of the infantry may also accompany the ski unit in the attack to effect the break-through. The nonski unit returns to its position after the penetration has been completed. The

point of leaving the enemy lines and the time the ski unit will arrive at that point must be known so that a break through may be effected for egress of the ski unit. It should be at some distance from the original break through for entrance unless special considerations warrant a decision to the contrary.

(3) The most favorable time for missions behind enemy lines is during the early evening hours. This affords the ski unit considerable time during which it may penetrate, under cover of darkness, far into the enemy's rear without being detected. Further actions depend on the mission. The principles of operations of raiding parties apply largely to actions behind the enemy lines.

(4) If adequate concealment, such as wooded terrain, is lacking, movements in the enemy's rear will usually be made only in darkness. The unit must be specially secured by a rear point and strong flank guards. During the day, troops should bivouac in remote, concealed positions. Inhabited places should be avoided. The bivouac area must be organized for all-around defense.

(5) Radio equipment may be the only means of communication with the main unit. Its use must be precisely prescribed in advance. In order to impede efforts of the enemy to search for and locate our radio equipment by radio-location finders, transmitting schedules and frequencies should be changed daily.

(6) For the return march, it is advisable to select a different route, which, if possible, will have been chosen and reconnoitered during the approach. If circumstances permit, friendly troops, if they were not advised before the operation, must be informed in advance of the manner and time of return. During the return march, as during the

approach march, it may be necessary to penetrate the enemy lines by attack from the rear. The unit then could not usually rely on effective support from the artillery and heavy weapons which have remained in position.

i. COMBAT AGAINST GUERRILLAS AND SPECIAL UNITS. Combat against enemy guerrilla bands, paratroops, and airborne troops in winter is one of the most essential tasks of the ski unit. Because of its great mobility in winter, the ski unit is able to locate an enemy quickly, and to annihilate him by systematically prepared surprise attacks. Destruction of hostile operating bases and shelters is the objective of the attacks.

56. Supply.

a. MEANS OF SUPPLY. (1) Methods of supplying ski units depend largely on the situation, the terrain, the condition of the winter roads, and snow and weather conditions. They may be different for each undertaking; hence the manner in which the troops will be supplied is stated precisely in every tactical order.

(2) The motor vehicles of the ski battalion trains, other than the cargo carrier M29 can take care of the supply of the fighting unit only so far as the enemy situation and the condition of winter roads permit. As a rule, it will be necessary to establish in the forward area a distributing point for companies.

(3) The company uses cargo carriers and tractor-drawn or hand-drawn sleds for its supply. Dog teams may prove useful.

(4) Supply trains should always be equipped with light machine guns and submachine guns. When necessary, they should be further protected by guard details.

b. SUPPLY POINTS. (1) The establishment of intermediate supply points depends on the length of the supply lines as well as on the difficulties of terrain and snow conditions. Often supply points must be set up even by small units (raiding parties and patrols), which, being absent for several days from their units while on special missions, cannot be supplied through regular supply channels and are unable to take the necessary supply of rations and ammunition along.

(2) Supply points must be prepared along the route of approach at such intervals that the distance between points or between supply point and receiving or distributing point, is not more than a day's march. If sufficient means of transportation are available, supply can be accelerated by shuttle traffic between points, and between supply points and receiving and distributing points, in which case the distance between the individual supply points should not exceed half a day's march.

(3) In the selection of sites, attention must be given to the storage of supplies in places which are well camouflaged, and protected as well as possible from frost. Best suited are shacks and small woods which are a short distance off the route of approach. In terrain threatened by the enemy, conditions may arise when supply points will have to be guarded continually and in adequate strength. If no special snow-shoveling details have been organized, guards should keep open the supply and approach routes in the vicinity of the supply points.

INDEX

259